THE
VANISHED
LIBRARY

This volume has benefited from
the collegial support of
The Wake Forest University Studium

Hellenistic Culture and Society
General Editors: Anthony W. Bulloch, Erich S. Gruen, A. A. Long,
and Andrew F. Stewart

THE
VANISHED
LIBRARY

Luciano Canfora

Translated by Martin Ryle

UNIVERSITY OF CALIFORNIA PRESS

Berkeley · Los Angeles

University of California Press
Berkeley and Los Angeles, California

First published by Hutchinson Radius 1989

© 1987 Sellerio editore via Siracusa 50 Palermo

Library of Congress Cataloging-in-Publication Data
Canfora, Luciano.
[Biblioteca scomparsa, English]
The vanished library / Luciano Canfora : translated by Martin Ryle.
p.   cm.
Translation of: La biblioteca scomparsa.
Includes index.
ISBN 0-520-07304-5 (cloth).—ISBN 0-520-07255-3 (paper)
1. Alexandria (Egypt). Library.   2. Libraries—Egypt—Alexandria—
History—to 400.   3. Alexandria (Egypt)—Intellectual life.
4. Alexandria (Egypt)—Antiquities.   5. Civilization, Classical.
I. Title.
Z722.5.C3513   1990
026.932—dc20
90-11087
CIP

Typeset by Selectmove Ltd, London
Printed in the United States of America
1 2 3 4 5 6 7 8 9

Contents

Chronology

264–241	First Punic War: Rome against Carthage.
260–253	Second Syrian War: Ptolemy II against Antiochus II and Antigonus Gonatas.
253	Peace between Egypt and Syria: Antiochus II marries Berenice, daughter of Ptolemy II.
250	Translation of the Jewish Bible into Greek at Alexandria by the Seventy (hence known as the 'Septuagint').
246–241	Third Syrian War (Ptolemy III against Seleucus II).
239	Death of Antigonus Gonatas.
229	Democratic revival in Athens.
227	Democratic reforms of Cleomenes at Sparta.
222	Battle of Sellasia, defeat of Cleomenes by the Macedonian king: Cleomenes flees to Egypt.
223–187	Antiochus III, 'the Great', on the throne of Syria.
219-217	Fourth Syrian War.
218–201	Second Punic War.
217	Victory of Ptolemy IV at Raphia over Antiochus.
215–205	First Macedonian War: Rome against Macedonia.
211	Death of Archimedes.
200	Antiochus III of Syria takes Judaea from Egypt.
196	Titus Quinctius Flamininus proclaims the freedom of Greece.
196	Foundation of Library at Pergamum.
190/189	Roman victory over Antiochus III at Magnesia.
188	Peace of Apamea between the Romans and Antiochus III.
180 ca.	Aristarchus publishes his edition of Homer, dividing the *Iliad* and *Odyssey* each into 24 parts – the basis of the modern text.
171–168	Macedonian war (Roman victory at Pydna): the historian Polybius becomes a hostage at Rome.
170–168	New outbreak of war between Egypt and Syria (Ptolemy VI and Antiochus IV).
166–164	Jewish revolt against Antiochus IV, led by Judas Maccabaeus.
164–163	Ptolemy VI flees Egypt; division of the kingdom between Ptolemy VI and the future Ptolemy VIII (Physcon).
155	Ptolemy VIII bequeaths his share of the kingdom to Rome.
149–146	Third Punic War.
147	Macedonia becomes a Roman province.

145	Death of Ptolemy VI.
145–116	Reign of Ptolemy VIII in Egypt.
134	Antiochus VII of Syria reconquers Jerusalem.
88	Uprising against the Romans at Ephesus and in all the province of Asia: 80,000 Romans killed. War between Sulla and Mithridates.
86	Victory of Sulla in Greece over the troops of Mithridates; conquest of Athens.
80–51	Reign of Ptolemy XII, 'the Piper'.
74–67	Third Mithridatic War.
67	Syria becomes a Roman province.
48	Battle of Pharsalus: Pompey flees into Egypt, where he is murdered.
48/47	Alexandrian war – Julius Caesar in Egypt.
44	Death of Caesar.
42	Battle of Philippi: Mark Antony defeats Brutus and Cassius.
37/36	Antony in Egypt: disastrous campaign against the Parthians.
31	Battle of Actium leaves Octavian as supreme ruler of Rome; fall of Alexandria; death of Cleopatra. Egypt becomes a province of Rome.
27	All of Greece becomes a province assigned to the Roman Senate.
17/19	Germanicus in the East.

A.D.

33	Death of Christ.
67	Nero frees Greece.
69	Vespasian at Alexandria.
128/129	Hadrian visits Athens and sponsors its library.
199/200	Septimius Severus grants Alexandria a Senate.
215	Caracalla's massacre at Alexandria.
267	Invasion of Greece by the Heruli.
270–275	Aurelian emperor of Rome; partially sacks Alexandria in his efforts to reconquer Egypt.
529	Justinian closes the School of Athens.
632	Death of Mohammed.
636	The Arabs take Syria.
639	The Arab conquest of Egypt begins.

PART I

I

The Pharaoh's Tomb

DURING the reign of Ptolemy Soter, Hecataeus of Abdera visited Egypt. He travelled up the Nile as far as the ancient capital, Thebes, renowned for its hundred gateways, each of them (so Homer had heard tell) wide enough to accommodate two hundred armed men together with their chariots and horses. The walls of the Temple of Ammon were still clearly visible, twenty-four feet thick and four hundred and five cubits (almost two hundred feet) high, and running for furlong after furlong. Within, everything lay in ruins, sacked by the troops of Cambyses, king of the Persians, who had swept down on Egypt in a demented frenzy of destruction: he had even deported the Egyptian artisans to Persia, planning to set them to work in the palaces of Susa and Persepolis. A little further on lay the royal tombs, of which only seventeen remained standing. In the valley of the queens, the priests showed Hecataeus the tomb of the concubines of Zeus, princesses of noble birth who in homage to the god were devoted to prostitution before marrying. A little further on rose an imposing mausoleum. This was the tomb of Rameses II, the pharaoh who had fought the Hittites in Syria: the Greek form of his name was Ozymandias.

Hecataeus went in, through an entrance hall sixty yards long and twenty yards high. Beyond this, he found himself in a square peristyle with sides some one hundred and twenty yards in length. The ceiling consisted of a single block of stone, dark blue in colour and glittering with stars. Columns twenty-five feet high supported this starry sky. These took the form of sculpted figures, each different from the next and each carved from a massive block of stone. As he moved on, Hecataeus took note of the building's plan. Now he stood before another doorway, similar to the one he had entered by but decorated in relief work and overlooked by three statues, each carved from a block of black stone.

The largest of the three (the largest statue of Egypt, so the priests assured him) towered over its neighbours, which reached only to its knees. This huge statue, whose feet were almost four yards long, represented Rameses. His mother stood at one knee and his daughter at the other. The ceiling, twenty-five feet high in the starry-skied hall, was all but lost to sight in here, and the visitor's disorientation was intensified by this unexpected change. Hecataeus was especially struck by the fact that the enormous statue of Rameses was carved from a single block, its surface unblemished by any scratch or mark. 'What is most admirable about this work', he noted, 'is not only its size, but above all the technique of its workmanship and the nature of the stone.' On the base was an inscription, which Hecataeus had translated into Greek: it read, 'I am Rameses, king of kings'. What followed was rather obscure: 'Whoever wishes to know how great I am and where I am to be

found, let him surpass one of my works.' The phrase was not without ambiguity. 'How great I am' might of course be a reference to size, an interpretation perhaps favoured by the fact that the words were inscribed at the feet of the huge statue – where, indeed, they might also seem to fulfil the pharaoh's promise to enlighten the beholder about 'where he was to be found'. And yet 'how great' might equally denote, by extension, not the statue's size but the grandeur of the 'works' which the inscription immediately went on to mention. And the other expression, 'where I am to be found', insofar as it invited or challenged the visitor to discover the sarcophagus, implicitly conveyed that its whereabouts were concealed and would be made known only to those who met certain conditions. The curiosity of the visitor was in any case confronted by a challenge and invited to a trial. There was further ambiguity in the formulation of this trial: 'surpass one of my works' (*nikato ti ton emon ergon*), or in other words accomplish – this seems to be the sense – works even greater than mine. If this was the correct interpretation, the text really amounted to a prohibition. Almost at the outset of his exploration, the visitor encountered this enormous apparition, which deterred him from searching for the sarcophagus. But perhaps the words could be understood differently? At all events, Hecataeus and his companions went on. Another statue, some thirty feet high, stood alone in the great hall: a woman, wearing three crowns. This enigmatic emblem was soon explained, for the priests told Hecataeus that she was the sovereign's mother, and her triple crown signified that she had been the daughter, the wife and the mother of a pharaoh.

The hall with the statues led into a peristyle decorated with bas-reliefs of the king's Bactrian campaign. The priests explained the historical and military background, telling Hecataeus that the royal army for the campaign had numbered some four hundred thousand infantry and twenty thousand cavalry, divided into four contingents each commanded by one of the king's sons. However, the priests did not always agree with one another in their elucidations of the bas-reliefs. For instance, one wall showed Rameses engaged in a siege, with the figure of a lion beside him. Hecataeus observed that:

> Some of the interpreters maintained that this was a real lion which the king had tamed and reared and which now faced the dangers of battle alongside its master; but others held that the king, whose unparalleled bravery was matched by his thirst for praise, had had himself portrayed beside the lion to show his boldness of spirit.

Hecataeus turned to the next wall, which showed the enemy defeated and taken captive. The figures had no hands and no genitals: this, it was explained, was because they had proved effeminate and feeble in the hour of battle. The third wall showed the king's triumphal return from the war and the sacrifices he had made in thanksgiving to the gods. The fourth wall, by contrast, was partly blocked off by the statues of two large seated figures, with three passageways opening immediately beside them.

This is the only occasion on which Hecataeus gives an explicit and detailed picture of how he made his way from one part of the building to the next. The three passages led into another wing, devoted not to the pharaoh's warlike exploits but to his works of peace.

II

The Sacred Library

H ECATAEUS tells us that he was given an explanation of the complicated route that led to Rameses'
sarcophagus. Had he found some way of eluding the
pharaoh's prohibition, or had he undergone the trial hinted
at in the teasingly-worded inscription? Or perhaps the
inscription no longer counted for anything, and was just
a curiosity displayed to those who visited the mausoleum?
Here is Hecataeus's account:

> The three passages led into a colonnaded hall, built on the plan
> of the Odeon and sixty yards in length. The room was filled
> with wooden statues of litigants, their eyes turned towards the
> judges whose figures were carved along one wall. There were
> thirty of these judges, and they had no hands. The supreme
> judge was placed in the middle. Truth hung about his neck,
> his eyes were shut, and scrolls lay piled around him on the
> floor. I was told that the bearing of these figures was intended
> to show that judges must not take gifts and that the supreme
> judge should have eyes only for the truth.
>
> Moving on, we entered a covered walk which gave access
> to chambers of every kind, decorated with reliefs showing a
> wealth of choice foods. Coloured bas-reliefs surrounded us as

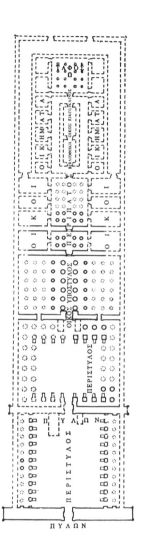

1. The Ramesseum at Thebes: reconstruction by Jollois and Devilliers, based on Diodorus.

9

we advanced; one showed the king offering to the divinities the gold and silver that flowed into his treasury each year from all the mines of Egypt. The total sum, thirty-two million *minae* of silver, was indicated below the bas-relief. There then followed the sacred library, above which were written the words: THE PLACE OF THE CURE OF THE SOUL. There followed images of all the Egyptian divinities, to each of which the king was offering some suitable gift, as if he wished to show Osiris and the lesser gods that he had lived in piety and justice towards men and gods all his life.

There was also a sumptuously built hall, the wall of which was contiguous with this library. Here there was a large table with twenty triclinia or couches, and statues of Zeus, Hera, and – once again – the king. It seems that the king's body had been buried here. All around the hall, they said, was a remarkable series of chambers, with splendid images of all the sacred animals of Egypt. By climbing up through these chambers, one might have reached the entrance of the tomb. This was on the roof of the building. There, too, a gold circle was to be seen, three hundred and sixty-five cubits long and one cubit high. Images for each day of the year were set out around this circle, one for every cubit: the rising and setting of the stars were recorded for each day, together with the signs with which those astral movements furnished the Egyptian astrologers. This frieze, they said, had been plundered by Cambyses when he made himself master of Egypt.

So runs Hecataeus's account in the transcription which Diodorus Siculus made two and a half centuries later. It seems, then, that Hecataeus reached no further than the library in his visit, and that from this point on his companions merely described or asked him to imagine the remainder. His descriptions certainly grow vaguer once we are past the library. It is not made clear, for instance, how he made his way from the library into the great hall with the triclinia: we are told only that the rooms shared a common wall. Moreover, the nature of the library itself is not immediately plain: one is struck by the particularly detailed description of how one of the reliefs, the one showing the Egyptian divinities and the pharaohs offering gifts to them, 'followed' the library.

Hecataeus recorded all this in his *History of Egypt*. He wrote this almost fictional work on concluding his travels, but it has not come down to us and we have to make do with that part of it copied by Diodorus. In his book, Hecataeus mingled ancient and modern, seeing ancient Egypt in terms of the new Ptolemaic reality; he confounded the old order with the contemporary dynasty of Ptolemy I. In a long digression, he gave an account of the Jews in Egypt and of Moses, a theme relevant to the life of the new Greek-Egyptian kingdom. He made his message still plainer by including an entire section designed to show how the best of the Greek law-givers had gone to Egypt in search of inspiration and learning. What better testimony could there be to the continuity between the old Egypt and the new? Ptolemy, highly appreciative of these labours, offered Hecataeus a diplomatic post, and he went to Sparta on his king's behalf.

Meanwhile, his book had become something of a travel guide. In course of time, Diodorus himself used it in this fashion. It was not, however, altogether reliable. A visitor to the mausoleum of Rameses would not have found

Hecataeus's descriptions entirely clear. It was strange, for instance, that in his account of the reliefs in the second peristyle he referred – perhaps, indeed, in a mere flight of exaggeration – to Rameses' wars in Bactria: how could the king have fought there? And what was one to make of the arrangement of covered walk, library and communal refectory which seemed to form an almost independent entity within the plan of the mausoleum? The expectant visitor would have been disappointed on entering this part of the monument, for the hall housing the library was nowhere to be found.

The Forbidden City

'EGYPT,' said the old beldame. 'Your husband is in Egypt.'

How better could she urge her master's suit, and persuade the lady to yield, than by invoking the splendours of that world-famed land? While the charming young lady was left alone at home in the island of Cos, her husband was no doubt amusing himself just as he pleased.

'There is nowhere in the world', she continued, 'that can show such wonders and delights as Egypt: gymnasia, pageants and spectacles, famous philosophers, money in heaps, fine young men, the sanctuary of the divine brother and sister. . . . The country is ruled by the most generous and noble of kings. Then there is the Museum; there are wines; there is every pleasure the gods can give. And as for the women, there are more of them than there are stars in the sky, and every one as beautiful as the goddesses Paris had to choose between in his famous judgement.'

The old go-between, predictably, had left the decisive factor to the end: surely the thought of these women would overcome the lady's resistance and persuade her to allow herself a little diversion of her own? Her list had started rather inconsequentially, though it had included one or two disturbing items. First the gymnasia, then the philosophers, and then – as if the thought was automatically suggested by the mention of those dubious friends of youth – the 'young men'; then, straying from her theme, she had spoken of the temple of Ptolemy and Arsinoe, of king Ptolemy, even of the Museum, before coming to what she hoped would be the most telling aspect: wine and women – women so numerous and so lovely that there could be little doubt how the lady's distant husband, from whom no word had been received for ten months, was employing his time.

During the feast of Adonis, the royal palace at Alexandria was opened to the public, and people flooded into the parks of the immense domain. Women sang songs in honour of Adonis, and had the lady of Cos been acquainted with their words ('our hair unbound, our garments untied, our breasts uncovered, we shall carry him to the bank where the waves foam'), they might have given her further grounds for anxiety. This feast was one of the rare occasions on which the palace was thrown open.

Travellers of antiquity used to say that Alexandria was shaped like a *chlamys*, an emperor's cloak. Its site was almost perfectly rectangular, and lay between the sea and the Mareotic Lake. The palace took up a fourth, perhaps even a third, of its area. As time passed, it grew even larger: Alexander had laid it out on the grand scale, and every one of his successors added some new building or monument.

As it expanded, the palace gradually occupied the entire district of the Bruchion. Its walls, protected by earthworks, overlooked the sea. It was a true fortress, designed to afford a last stronghold in times of exceptional danger: during the 'Alexandrian war', Caesar barricaded himself in the building with a small band of armed men and succeeded for several days in withstanding the siege of the Egyptian armies. The notion of an inaccessible palace (inaccessible, that is, to everyone but the descendants of the seven families who had foiled the conspiracy of the Magi), derived from Persia, had entered Hellenistic royal tradition by way of Alexander. The court of the Ptolemies in Egypt also inherited certain customs of the long-dead pharaohs.

Outsiders can have had only a vague idea of what lay within the palaces of the royal quarter. It was known, for instance, that the 'Museum' must be there, and we have seen that the go-between on Cos included this 'Museum' among the marvels of Alexandria – very likely without knowing what it was. There were also precious collections of books belonging to the king, called 'the royal books' by Aristeas, a Jewish writer familiar with both the palace and the library.

IV

The Fugitive

THE waspish Crates was the last person he would have chosen to meet with – especially in such wretched circumstances, and in so unfriendly a place as Thebes. But since it was impossible to avoid him, he went up to him. Crates, however, proved surprisingly amiable. He began by making some general remarks about the lot of the exile, which he regarded as by no means painful. In fact, it was a welcome escape from the many annoyances and surprises of politics.

'Take heart, Demetrius,' he said in conclusion. 'Have faith in yourself and in your new position.'

Demetrius had governed Athens for ten years, during which time he had seen hundreds of statues raised in his honour. He now found himself in Thebes, escaping from the new ruler of Athens, whom they called *poliorcetes*, the 'besieger of cities', in ironic allusion to his stubborn and often unsuccessful military campaigns. Taken aback by his interlocutor's unexpectedly courteous demeanour, but quick to recover his poise, Demetrius returned to his friends, saying half in jest and half in earnest, 'A curse on politics, then, since it has stopped me from making the

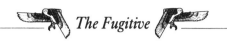

acquaintance of this man before today.' Naturally he took no notice of Crates' advice – advice that was nothing less than a warning from the gods, as became clear to those able to recall this strange meeting many years later. He left Thebes as soon as he could, and presented himself in Alexandria. Here, at the court of Ptolemy, he spent the last part of his life as a counsellor to the king.

In days gone by, Philip of Macedon had wanted Aristotle to be tutor to Alexander. Ptolemy, the first monarch of Egypt, would have liked Aristotle's follower Theophrastus to teach his favourite son: but Theophrastus had remained in Athens, sending Ptolemy the accomplished scholar Strato in his stead (Strato in fact eventually succeeded Theophrastus). The Lagian dynasty had Macedonian antecedents, and took particular pride in its direct descent from Philip (Ptolemy encouraged the story that Philip had been his real father, and Theocritus develops this theme in his *Encomium* of Ptolemy); it thus enjoyed a certain hereditary relationship with the Aristotelian school. Indeed, Aristotle's father had been the personal physician of the Macedonian king.

This explains why Demetrius decided on Alexandria, for he too had belonged to the school, having been a pupil of Aristotle and a friend of Theophrastus. When governor of Athens he had shown great favour to its members and alumni, who formed a select and rather unpopular group. Now that his protector Cassander had fallen into adversity, dragging his protégé down with him, Demetrius took refuge with the Ptolemies. The Ptolemies were moreover related to Cassander and to his father Antipater, 'regent' of Macedonia after the death of Alexander. Demetrius took

Aristotelian methods with him to Egypt, and they were the key to his success. The methods that had put the Peripatetic school in the forefront of western learning were followed in Alexandria, in the grand style and under royal patronage. Before long people were saying that 'Aristotle had taught the kings of Egypt how to organise a library': the apparent anachronism concealed a real truth. Demetrius was also said to have urged Ptolemy to 'collect together books on kingship and the exercise of power, and to read them'. He became so intimate with the king that he was called 'the first of his friends', and was even credited with inspiring the laws enacted by Ptolemy.

Once he had reached these heights, Demetrius, led by his love of intrigue, began to meddle in dynastic politics. Here too he tried to guide the king's hand. Ptolemy had children by his marriage to Eurydice, and four children by Berenice, a much-travelled and fascinating widow who was a native of Cyrene. Berenice had arrived in Alexandria in company with Eurydice, and all three had lived together at court in perfect amity. However, Ptolemy began to favour one of his four children by Berenice, and at length proposed to share the throne with him, much to Eurydice's distress. Demetrius, motivated perhaps by the fact that she was Antipater's daughter, took it upon himself to interfere on Eurydice's behalf in this delicate affair. He may well have felt that Ptolemy was not likely to go through with a dynastic alliance that would connect him with a family of local landowners instead of with the rulers of Macedonia. He began to utter hints and warnings, taking what he thought would prove an effective line: 'If you give place to someone else,

you will find yourself empty-handed.' However, his rather petty arguments fell on deaf ears. Ptolemy had made up his mind to seat his favourite son on the throne beside him. Eurydice, realising that there was no more to be done, left Egypt in despair.

Soon afterwards, early in the year 285, the young Ptolemy officially took his place beside his father. For three years they shared the kingdom, and then Ptolemy I Soter died. His successor, now sole ruler, addressed himself to the question of how best to be rid of Demetrius. He had him arrested, or at least placed under surveillance, while he was making up his mind. And so the wheel had turned full circle, and Demetrius was no better off than in those wretched Theban days, when Crates had spoken the far-seeing but ineffectual warning which he, Demetrius, had smiled at and ignored.

Still under strict surveillance, he was despatched to a remote village inland. As he lay dozing there one day, he felt a sudden stab of pain in his right hand, which dangled beside him as he drowsed. In the brief moment that elapsed before he died, he realised a serpent had bitten him. Ptolemy, it was quite clear, had arranged to have him killed.

V

The Universal Library

DEMETRIUS had been in charge of the library. From time to time the king would enquire about his books, rather as if he were reviewing his troops: 'How many scrolls do we have now?', he would ask, and Demetrius would give him the latest figure. They had a particular goal in view, for they had calculated that they must amass some five hundred thousand scrolls altogether if they were to collect at Alexandria 'the books of all the peoples of the world'. Ptolemy composed a letter 'to all the sovereigns and governors on earth', imploring them 'not to hesitate to send him' works by authors of every kind: 'poets and prose-writers, rhetoricians and sophists, doctors and soothsayers, historians, and all the others too'. He gave orders that any books on board ships calling at Alexandria were to be copied: the originals were to be kept, and the copies given to their owners. The collection thus acquired was known as the 'ships' collection'.

On occasion, Demetrius would draw up a written report for his sovereign. 'Demetrius to the great king', it would begin:

In pursuance of your order that the collections of the library should be enlarged and made complete by the addition of those books still lacking, and that those which are imperfect should be properly restored, I have taken great pains, and I now submit this account of my proceedings. . . .

In one of these accounts, Demetrius suggested that 'the books of the Jewish law' should be acquired. 'These books, in their correct form, really should be included in your library', he argued. Here he invoked the authority of Hecataeus of Abdera, certain that this would favourably impress the king. In his *History of Egypt*, Hecataeus had devoted a good deal of space to Jewish history. His reasons for doing so, as reported by Demetrius, were rather curious: 'It is no wonder', Hecataeus had argued,

> that authors, poets and the common run of historians have failed to refer to these books and to the men who have lived and still live, in accordance with them: if they have been passed over in silence, that is not by chance, but because of the sacred matter that they contain.

When the number of scrolls had reached 200,000, and Ptolemy was paying another visit to the library, Demetrius returned to his theme. He had been informed, he told the king, that the Jewish laws were also books worth copying and including in the library.

'Very well,' replied Ptolemy. 'What hinders you from seeing to the business? You know that you can give orders for whatever you need in the way of men and materials.'

'But the books must be translated,' said Demetrius. 'They are not written in Syriac, as is generally believed, but in Hebrew, an altogether different language.'

The witness who reports this dialogue, assuring us that he heard it with his own ears, was one of the large and active Jewish community established in the royal district. The Jews of Alexandria had settled in an area said to have been allocated to them by Alexander himself (the grammarian Apion, a hardened anti-Semite, complained that it was the finest part of the whole quarter). Our witness was completely Hellenized in language and culture, and his enterprising spirit had led him to take advantage of this perfect camouflage to enter the royal court, where he had won esteem and made friends. The question of whether the Greek language should be employed for divine service in the synagogue, a practice by that time prevalent but still opposed by those of more orthodox beliefs, was much debated among Alexandrian Jews, and he too was concerned about the problem. We can assume that he was able to avail himself of the presence at court of co-religionists or sympathisers, and that this was how he obtained a post in the library. From what he writes, we can infer that he successfully concealed his membership of the Jewish community, and that he continued to speak and write about the Jews as if they were an interesting but alien people.

He discusses writing materials and the making of scrolls with much expertise and technical exactitude. As a zealous and valuable *diaskeuastes* (curator of texts), we can imagine that he became an increasingly close confidant of Demetrius, and may well have encouraged him to put before the king, respectfully but repeatedly, the suggestion that the Jewish laws should be given a place on the shelves of the royal library.

In all this, however, we must indeed rely in part on our imaginations, for our author says rather little about himself. He tells us that his name is Aristeas and that he has a brother called Philocrates: both names are thoroughly Greek, but they may not have been unusual among the Jews of the diaspora, who were every year more affected by the 'Hellenism' which their orthodox fellow-Jews deplored. He tells us, too, that he was on friendly terms with the two captains of Ptolemy's bodyguard, Sosibius of Tarentum and Andrew; that he was present during the colloquy between Demetrius and the king on the library premises (a conversation whose first part we have already reported); and that he took part in the mission Ptolemy sent to Jerusalem in search of capable translators. He also lets it be understood that he is the same Aristeas who had written a book called *Who the Jews Are* – based, so he insists, entirely on information given by Egyptian priests, just like the excursus to Hecataeus's *History of Egypt*. Here again, though this time the device is hardly credible, he endeavours to pass as a 'gentile'. In cases of this kind, it is hard to judge whether accusations of 'collaborating' are exaggerated and unfair, or whether they are in part justified. If we go by the result (which is certainly one possible criterion), we can hardly deny that Aristeas' initiative greatly benefited the Jews. However, no-one can conceal the advantage that their rulers drew from a better knowledge of their subjects.

In saying that the books of the Jewish law were 'also' worth translating, Demetrius had implied that this would not be the first such task undertaken in the library. We read in a Byzantine treatise that learned men were enlisted from every nation, men who as well as being masters of their own languages were wonderfully well acquainted with Greek. Each group of scholars was allocated the appropriate texts, and so a Greek translation of every text was made.

The translation of the Iranian writings attributed to Zoroaster, amounting to more than two million lines of verse, was remembered centuries later as a notable feat: when Callimachus compiled a classified catalogue of the Greek authors, his pupil Hermippus set out to match him (perhaps, in his own private estimation, to outdo him) by making an index to these two million lines, compared to which the *Iliad* and the *Odyssey*, with their few score thousand hexameters, were little more than breviaries. These scholars were privileged to imagine that they might actually gather together every book in the world – a glittering mirage, which cast its spell on the library for a while before becoming the stuff of literary fantasy. This desire for completeness, this will to power, are akin to the impulse which drove Alexander, as a rhetorician of antiquity put it, 'to overstep the limits of the world'. Alexander was also said to have planned a vast library at Nineveh, for which he had arranged for Chaldaean texts to be translated.

The Ptolemies and their librarians set out not only to collect every book in the world, but to translate them all into Greek. Naturally, Greek compendia and compilations were also prepared, one example being the *Egyptian History* of Manetho, a priest from Sebennytus in the Delta region who worked at Heliopolis. Manetho used scores of different sources, including scrolls kept in temples and lists of kings and their exploits – just as Megasthenes, the ambassador of king Seleucus of Syria to the court of Pathaliputra, had done in his Indian researches.

Macedonian arms had made the Greeks masters of the entire known world, from Sicily to North Africa, from the Balkan peninsula to Asia Minor, and from Iran and India to Afghanistan, where Alexander had halted. They did not learn the languages of their new subjects, but they realised that if they were to rule them they must understand them, and that to understand them they must collect their books and have them translated. Royal libraries were accordingly created in all the Hellenistic capitals, not just for the sake of prestige but also as instruments of Greek rule. And the sacred books of the subject peoples had a special place in this systematic project of collection and translation, because religion was, for those who wished to rule them, a kind of gateway to their souls.

 VI

'I leave my books to Neleus'

THEOPHRASTUS, who died sometime between 288 and 284 BC, left a will containing one rather strange clause: 'I leave all my books to Neleus'. He bequeathed 'the garden and the covered way, and the buildings near the garden' to the other scholars. (He was able to do so because Demetrius, when ruler of Athens, had at last made it possible for him to gain possession, despite his lack of Athenian citizenship, of the land on which the school was built.) His books, however, were for Neleus alone. Why was this man singled out for the privilege? And what 'books' did Theophrastus mean?

Neleus, a native of the Asian city of Scepsis, in Troas, was probably by this time the only man alive who had been taught by Aristotle in person. He was the son of Coriscus – the same Coriscus whom Aristotle used to mention when, in the course of his teaching, he wished to indicate that he was referring to a concrete subject. On the death of Plato, Neleus had left the Academy along with Aristotle and had accompanied him to Assus, not far from Scepsis. Here they had been received by a local nobleman, Hermias, a former slave and a eunuch, who had achieved some influence through his close links with Philip of Macedon. He was a fifth columnist on Philip's behalf in the Persian empire. Then someone betrayed him, and the king of Persia seized him and put him to the torture, though without extracting any useful information from him. His death moved Aristotle to write an anthem, the Hymn to Virtue, expressing his sorrow and admiration. Aristotle had close links with this world, for on the death of his father Nicomachus he had been looked after by his tutor, Proxenus of Atarneus, a compatriot of Coriscus and Hermias. Thus Neleus, as well as being a friend of Aristotle's, came from a part of the world that had meant a great deal to him. Theophrastus had therefore assumed, not unreasonably, that Neleus would succeed him as head of the School; and he had accordingly left to Neleus in person the precious bequest of 'Aristotle's books'.

These, it would seem, were volumes compiled from Aristotle's lectures, on the basis and in the course of his teaching and with the active involvement of his students. Each was unique, and together they formed an irreplaceable testimony to a process of creative reflection never set down in books intended for the world at large. Since these invaluable texts would find their true use in the School, it was fitting that they should be entrusted to the personal care and authority of its probable future head.

However, Neleus was not elected head. The School had seen many changes in the years since Demetrius's flight to Egypt. Under the quasi-democratic regime of Poliorcetes, the 'Besieger of Cities', life cannot have been easy for the former protégés of his predecessor Demetrius Phalereus. In the event, Strato was elected – the same Strato who had visited the court of the Ptolemies as tutor to the royal heir, a connection which may well have helped him win the election. Neleus retired in dudgeon to his birthplace, Scepsis, taking with him the precious books entrusted to his care. This loss, impossible to make good, was a heavy blow to the School. The general principles of the master's thought were known, of course, and there was an abundance of paraphrases. Theophrastus, in point of fact, had written several paraphrases – rather prolix ones – and whenever he chanced on a new thought of his own, he took care to swaddle it in voluminous Aristotelian drapery. What the School had been deprived of by Neleus's abrupt departure was something different: the actual unravelling of an idea, the interlinking of a chain of inferences, as these had been worked out in the labour of successive years. Here, the characteristic Aristotelian method had been employed. The same subjects, approached anew after a lapse of time, yielded fresh reflections: strictly speaking, these should have effaced what had gone before, but those who had listened and contributed to the great work of intellectual construction had preferred to add them to the earlier layers of thought. Too scrupulously pious to erase a word, and perhaps too prudent also, these disciples had done homage to Aristotle by creating a mosaic or jigsaw puzzle which it would fall to others, centuries later, to piece together. For the moment, the philosophers of the Peripatetic School could only 'formulate general principles'. They had no alternative, joked the learned grammarian Tyrannion, but to repeat empty, bombastic generalities. This was why such men as Zeno and Epicurus, who had come to Athens as twenty-year-olds at the time of Aristotle's death, encountered only his least original work, which he himself had published during his lifetime in the familiar Platonic form of the dialogue.

Neleus's haughty departure to Troas with the living record of the master's words was not likely to pass unremarked, especially at a time when Ptolemy Philadelphus had decided to create his universal library. Ptolemy had every reason to expect that his former tutor, now head of the School, would be able to help him in his grand design. Strato, however, with the best will in the world, could only advise his old pupil the king to apply to the ill-humoured Neleus. Neleus was accordingly sought out, in the hope that money might succeed where his fellow-peripatetics' appeals to his loyalty had failed. Neleus, however, duped the Egyptian king's messengers, selling them various unimportant treatises, a quantity of Theophrastus's works (no rarities, these), and above all a number of books which had *belonged to* Aristotle. This was a play on words. Yes, Neleus agreed, the royal messengers were rightly informed: he did have in his possession 'Aristotle's library' – the collection of books, that is, which Aristotle had owned. He was prepared to part with these, he said, though he did so with reluctance.

At first, the Alexandrians did not realise they had been taken in. An entry in the library catalogue recorded the acquisition, 'during the reign of Ptolemy Philadelphus', of 'the books of Aristotle and Theophrastus, from Neleus of Scepsis'.

VII

The Symposium

ARISTEAS took full advantage of circumstances. When
Ptolemy agreed to the suggestion that the Jewish law
should be translated, he at once pressed him to answer a
difficult question. The Jewish law, he pointed out, which
they had just agreed to have not only copied out but translated, was observed by the Hebrew people everywhere. How
was it that even while this project was being undertaken,
many Jews lay in Ptolemy's prisons?

Aristeas had chosen his moment carefully. Sosibius of
Tarentum and Andrew, captains of the royal bodyguard,
were with the king, and Aristeas had already canvassed their
views and won their support for his request. The subtlety of
his approach makes one wonder whether he had not actually
had the translation suggested – for the suggestion, given
Ptolemy's ambition, was certain to be taken up – purely so
as to be able to point out the inconsistency between such a
project and the treatment meted out to the deported Jews.

Aristeas paid the expected tribute to the king's generous
disposition, and then waited in silence for his reaction.

The conversation which followed seemed for a moment
to echo the earlier discussion about the scrolls. 'How many

thousand do you think there are?' Ptolemy asked Andrew (but he meant Jews, not scrolls).

Andrew, by no means unprepared for the question, had his answer ready: 'Rather more than a hundred thousand.'

'So it's only a small favour that Aristeas is asking,' was Ptolemy's ironic comment.

He was prepared to grant the request, however, since it met with the approval of his two most loyal retainers. The prisoners were freed and their owners compensated from the funds of the 'royal bank'. Those captured by Ptolemy Soter in the course of his Syrian campaign were not the only beneficiaries: the arrangement also applied to all Jews already resident in Egypt at that time, or who had been deported there before or after the campaign. The edict granting them their freedom declared: 'We are persuaded that the enslavement of these people took place against our father's will and against all propriety, and came about through the unruly conduct of the soldiery.' Its terms thus avoided any disavowal of the late king's actions.

The freeing of the deported Jews established Ptolemy's credentials with Eleazar, the high priest of Jerusalem. In a message requesting that expert translators be sent to Alexandria, the Egyptian king announced:

> We have set free more than one hundred thousand Jews. The sturdiest have been enrolled in the army. Those fitted to work alongside us, and worthy of the trust that a courtier enjoys, have been given administrative positions. . . . We have resolved to do what will please all the Jews: those we have mentioned, those in other parts of the world, and all those who may come here in the

future. For we have decided to have your laws translated from Hebrew into Greek, so that they may take
their place in our library beside the rest of the king's
books.

Eleazar responded enthusiastically to the king's proposal,
greeting him as a 'sincere friend' and sending good wishes
to him, to his sister-wife Arsinoe, and to their children.
Ptolemy's letter was read out in public, we are informed by
Aristeas, who led the Alexandrian delegation jointly with his
friend Andrew.

His visit to Jerusalem left a strong impression on Aristeas:
he was much struck, for instance, by the sight of the high
priest in all his solemn and splendid pomp, and as a Jew
of the diaspora he must have been moved by this encoun-
ter with his roots. Jerusalem seemed very small compared
with the great city of Alexandria where he had always
lived. With his usual prudent good sense, he made this
the starting-point for some rather complacent and indul-
gent reflections on the domestic policy of the Ptolemies.
If (he reasoned) the rural population in Egypt – in other
words, the native population – was forbidden to remain
more than twenty days in the towns, this was explained
and justified by the sovereign's heartfelt desire to preserve
agriculture from the decay which would threaten it if too
many peasants moved to the city. Aristeas took the view
that the Jews and the Greeks were destined to command,
while the Egyptians must be kept in their place. Ptolemy
had expressed exactly the same opinion when he had written to Eleazar, telling him that a considerable number of
Jews had been made garrison commanders, at good rates

of pay, 'so as to strike fear into the hearts of the Egyptian race'.

A delegation of seventy-two learned Jews, six from each of the twelve tribes of Israel, set out for Egypt, where Ptolemy welcomed them with a warmth which set the seal on this rapprochement between the two ruling races. The banquet in their honour lasted for seven days. Ptolemy seized the chance to further his political education by embarking on a series of subtle casuistical discussions in which no aspect of kingship, not even the most trivial, was left untouched. Demetrius's advice that he should 'acquire books on kingship and read them' was evidently bearing fruit.

The assembled sages were subjected to a volley of questions, ten every day. 'How can the kingdom be preserved?' asked Ptolemy. 'How can one obtain the agreement of one's friends? In legal proceedings, how can one win the assent of people who fail to see the truth? How can one bequeath one's kingdom intact to one's heirs? How are unforeseen events to be borne with equanimity?' – and much more besides.

To each of these questions, the learned Jews would find a reply at once respectful, original, and consistent with their opinion that God's omnipotence extended into the furthest recesses of human life. One of those present on the first day of the banquet was Menedemus of Eretria, a Greek philosopher, a dialectician who had attended the Platonic Academy and had subsequently joined the Megarean school of his master, Stilpon. Menedemus, who was present as a representative of the king of Cyprus, had no intention of taking part in these debates: he found them, to tell the truth, somewhat peculiar.

'What is the acme of courage?' Ptolemy would eagerly enquire. Then he would ask: 'How can one make sure of sleeping undisturbed?' or 'How does one succeed in thinking only good thoughts?' The questions continued: 'How can one escape from grief? How does one learn to listen to what others have to say? What is the grossest form of negligence? How can one stay on good terms with one's wife?'

Even this last question did not dismay the wise old men. 'Given that the female sex is bold and headstrong,' one of their number replied, 'and given especially that women, while there is no restraining them in pursuit of what they desire, are easily distracted by false reasoning, it follows that one should always deal with them deliberately and dispassionately, and always avoid provoking quarrels. The way lies plain enough, so long as the traveller knows where he wants to go. Moreover, whoever calls upon God is sure to find the right path through all life's problems.'

'And how should one employ one's leisure?'

'You should read,' answered one of the old men, unaware perhaps that his interlocutor owned all the world's books. 'Above all, you should read the accounts of those who have travelled in the various kingdoms of the world. This will help you to watch over the security of your subjects. If you succeed in that, you will win glory and God will grant your wishes.'

Ptolemy turned to Menedemus, curious to know what he thought. 'You see,' he remarked, 'even when taken unawares by questions of all kinds, they answer in accordance with reason, and they all make God the mainspring of their reasoning.'

'Yes, your Majesty,' replied Menedemus, adroitly avoiding any expression of dissent. 'If we assume that everything depends on the force of providence, and make it a premise that man is God's creature, then indeed it must follow that every reasoned argument traces its vigour and beauty back to God.'

'Exactly,' Ptolemy said in conclusion, not realising that Menedemus had actually avoided expressing any opinion of his own. And here the discussion ended, according to Aristeas' informant, and 'everybody betook themselves to gaiety'.

At this time, the theatres of Alexandria (of which there were still some four hundred at the period of the Arab siege) were presenting a series of gaudy historical playlets, designed to suit the taste of the various peoples who mingled in the city's cosmopolitan streets. The Greeks, many of whom came from the city-states of Asia, particularly enjoyed a play based on the story of Gyges as told by Herodotus – a mediocre travesty, which predictably enjoyed a long run thanks to the titillating episode in which Candaules, smitten with his wife's beauty, forces his minister to hide in the bedroom and watch the queen undressing. Some people amused themselves by making copies of certain scenes. In the theatres that the Jews attended, there was a fashion for the so-called 'tragedies' of Ezekiel, a talented scene-shifter who produced dramatisations of the best-known and most exciting incidents of the Old Testament. These consisted of tableaux with choric commentaries, representing the story of Moses, the flight into Egypt, and the Babylonian captivity. Such subjects appealed to a taste rather different from that which enjoyed harem stories after Herodotus, and a number of Greek authors were bold enough to attempt versions of their own. One of these was Theodectes of Phaselis, who scored a resounding failure.

However, now that the sages of Jerusalem, the fine flower of rabbinical learning, were in Alexandria, efforts were made to stop the staging of these passages from sacred history, which mingled the holy and the profane and which the visitors made it plain that they strongly disliked. The plays, moreover, were naturally written in Greek, the usual language even of those Jews who enjoyed such entertainments, and it seemed almost offensive that underhand and scarcely reliable stage versions should be in circulation at the very moment when the scholars were commencing work in an atmosphere of solemn piety on the keenly awaited Greek translation of the Pentateuch. It was wrong to tolerate such confusion – worse confounded, as Demetrius had reported to the king, by the fact that more or less worthless unauthorised Greek translations of the 'holy' scriptures were already available.

Surprisingly, perhaps, the seventy-two sages were not accommodated in the Museum. They were given quarters on the little island of Pharos, some seven stadia from the city, and here they set to work. As the translation progressed, Demetrius and his assistants would collect the text agreed by the scholars and make a definitive transcription of it. The seventy-two translators completed their task in seventy-two days.

 VIII

In the Cage of the Muses

IN the Museum, however, life was far from quiet. 'In the populous land of Egypt,' sneered a poet of the time, 'they breed a race of bookish scribblers who spend their whole lives pecking away in the cage of the Muses.' Timon, the sceptical philosopher to whom we owe these words, knew that the fabled Museum was to be found in Alexandria (or rather, 'in Egypt': he is vague on this point). He calls it 'the cage of the Muses' because he sees its denizens as rare birds, remote and precious creatures 'bred' by the Egyptians – an allusion to the material privileges granted them by the king: they received free meals and a stipend, and were exempt from taxation.

They are 'scribblers', *charakitai*, because they scribble on rolls of papyrus: in Greek, there is a play on words, for *charax* is 'an enclosure' – the pen within which these fancy birds live their mysterious lives. We would be no worse off without them, Timon believes: all their aura of secrecy and mystery is a mere camouflage to cover their nullity and emptiness. To prove his point, he advises his frequent companion Aratus, author of the *Phenomena*, to consult the 'old copies' of Homer rather than the 'latest correct editions'. This is a contemptuous allusion to the labours of Zenodotus of Ephesus, the first librarian of the Museum, on the texts of the *Iliad* and the *Odyssey*. Zenodotus had introduced a new reading, for instance, in Book IV, line 88 of the *Iliad*, where Athena is shown amidst the Trojan heroes 'trying to find the godlike Pandarus, wherever he might be': it was impossible, argued Zenodotus, that a goddess should be shown 'having to search for the object of her quest'. He had also proposed to delete the fourth and fifth lines of the first book, the famous lines that refer to the bodies of the dead Achaeans as 'carrion for the dogs and birds', but his grounds for rejecting them fortunately failed to convince anybody else. One can understand Timon's impatience with this kind of thing.

Of course the librarians did not spend all their time in such wilful meddling. Classification, subdivision into books, the making of new copies, annotation: there was work enough on the ever-growing collection of material, which was further swollen by the scholars' own ponderous commentaries. Only a few of the staff really knew every highway and byway of the library. During one of the poetry competitions which the Ptolemies liked to stage from time to time (we are now in the reign of Ptolemy Euergetes), the king turned to the élite of the Museum to advise him on the selection of a seventh member for the panel of judges. They suggested a certain Aristophanes, a scholar of Byzantine origin, whose 'only pastime', they said, was to 'read and reread his way carefully through every book in the library in the order in which they are arranged'. Aristophanes, then, must surely know this sequence to perfection. He was soon to demonstrate as much, unmasking the plagiarism of the contenders for the top poetry prizes when he left the jury in the midst of its deliberations and made his way to the library, where (so Vitruvius tells us in his account of the affair) he 'relied upon his memory' to guide him to certain shelves 'well known to him', and shortly reappeared brandishing the original texts which the plagiarists had tried to pass off as their own.

Callimachus attempted an overall classification, sub-dividing his *Catalogues* into generic categories correspond-ing to the various sections of the library. His vast work, which itself took up some 120 scrolls, was entitled *Catalogues of the authors eminent in various disciplines*. It did give an idea of the system by which the library's scrolls were arranged, but it was certainly not a plan or guide: such plans were not produced until much later, in the time of Didymus. Callimachus's *Catalogues* were of use only to someone already familiar with the arrangement of the material. Moreover, since their basic idea was to list only those authors 'eminent' in the various branches of literature, they represented no more than a selection – albeit a very extensive one – from the complete catalogue. Callimachus devoted six sections to poetry and five to prose: his catego-ries included epics, tragedies, comedies, historical works, works of medicine, rhetoric and law, and miscellaneous works.

The spirit of Aristotle patrolled these shelves of well-ordered scrolls. Demetrius had transplanted to the soil of Alexandria the master's conception of a community of learned men isolated from the outside world and equipped with a complete library and a retreat where they could cultivate the Muses, and Strato's long sojourn at court had helped it to take firm root. 'The organisation of the library', a French scholar has commented, 'reveals the method and the spirit of the far-off Stagirite.' The shelves which should have housed the Aristotelian texts were a painful sight, however. They contained almost nothing but those works issued by Aristotle in his lifetime – apart, that is, from spurious texts which had crept into the canon, and which were to prove very difficult to dislodge. The major works, the *Treatises* (as they were called in the School), were virtually unrepresented. And the lack of these *Treatises* was becoming more and more conspicuous as lists drawn up by people connected with the School began to circulate: these may have been no more than crude enumerations of titles, but they made it quite clear that Neleus had perpetrated a notable hoax. The proliferation of such lists also increased the risk that works would be shelved in error, since (as that incomparable bibliophile John Philoponus noted centuries later) there was no shortage of books whose titles were the same even though they had been written by other authors, such as Eudemus, Phanias and Theophrastus himself, to mention only the best known. There was no shortage, either, of works by other authors called Aristotle, who might be confused in the heat of the moment with the Stagirite. And Ptolemy Euergetes was determined to amass a complete collection of Aristotle, in rivalry, it was said, with the king of Libya, a passionate collector of Pythagoras's works.

Aristotle's teaching, however, remained well known, especially in its critical and literary aspects (and leaving aside the biographical essay form which the Peripatetics may be said to have invented). It had been transmitted, admittedly, by way of the elaborations and reworkings of members of the School, beginning with Demetrius's own treatises *On the Iliad, On the Odyssey* and *On Homer*. In this field, it might even have been claimed that Aristotle offered the only systematic theoretical approach, of especial value because it was based not on vague intuitions but on a collection of actual texts. Aristotle's collection, limited though it was to what he had been able to acquire for himself, allowed him to develop a method quite different from the extravagant procedures of his master, Plato, who had been ready to hold forth on poetry but whose familiarity with actual poems was a matter of considerable uncertainty: once, after all, wanting to refer to the poems of Antimachus, he had had to wait for months and months while a copy was brought to him from Asia Minor.

Nor had Aristotle been given to childish excesses such as banning Homer from the 'ideal City'. He had drawn up a sensible classification, distinguishing between the *Iliad* and the *Odyssey* on one hand and the poems of the epic cycle on the other; and he had persuasively explained why the former two poems, each constructed around a single episode, excelled the others, which were mere concatenations of events lacking any centre. This basic distinction was central to Demetrius's argument in his Homeric treatises, and it became a point of dogma for the learned men of the Museum. Zenodotus accepted it quite without discussion, and deduced on its basis that while Homer was the sole author of the two celebrated poems, all the rest were to be attributed to other writers. Aristarchus, the 'hyper-critic', took the same view a century later, dismissing as no more than a 'paradox' the view, held by Xenon and others, that the author of *The Iliad* was 'separate' from the author of *The Odyssey*. And Callimachus, although as an artist he had little time for some of Aristotle's theories, was quick to proclaim his orthodoxy on this point: 'I hate cyclical poems,' he wrote in an epigram, 'since I cannot bear a road which swerves all over the place.' This was a statement in verse of Aristotle's theory that the cyclical poems, motley patchworks of incident, lacked true unity.

However, this rather exaggerated doctrinal zeal masked a certain impatience on Callimachus's part with the doctrine of the 'single and continuous' narrative. He complained, polemically, that 'the Telchines chirp against me like cicadas because I haven't written one continuous poem thousands of lines long'. 'Telchines', 'a cannibal tribe ready to eat your liver out', maleficent demons: in such terms Callimachus railed at the rivals and adversaries by whom he felt surrounded in the Museum. Although he is not mentioned by name, Apollonius, director of the library until the death of Ptolemy Philadelphus, was certainly one of Callimachus's targets. Apollonius had written a ponderous poem in four books, each of them running to several thousand lines, centred on the story of Jason and Medea but swollen by the inclusion of every detail of the narrative background, including a full account of the whole voyage of the Argonauts in quest of the fleece. Callimachus had paid assiduous homage to Ptolemy Philadelphus, writing celebratory verses on his marriage to his sister Arsinoe and on the subsequent apotheosis of the queen, but Apollonius had continued to enjoy the sovereign's good graces and had retained the prestigious post of 'librarian'. In a sense, it was on Apollonius's orders that Callimachus had to toil away at his *Catalogues*: the reflection is unlikely to have sweetened his temper. Callimachus's learning was not in question (although Aristophanes later devoted an entire critical essay to the shortcomings of his *Catalogues,* and although some of his ideas in the vexed matter of the attribution of orations and tragedies seemed frankly arbitrary). As a poet, however, he was unacceptably modern. He could be needlessly sensual on occasion, as when he made Tiresias's sighting of the goddess in her bath the central motif of his hymn to Pallas. This, people must have felt, resembled certain Hebrew erotic poems, rather than the formal stiffness of Apollonius's Medea. In his almost ostentatious search for novelty, Callimachus was prepared to take his inspiration from the Hebrew literature recently translated into Greek, rendering some verses of Isaiah in the form of an epigram in elegiac distichs.

Tensions such as these were resolved, in the end, from above, for the rare birds in the Muses' cage belonged to the sovereign. Vitruvius tells us that when the sophist Zoilus came to Alexandria to recite his contemptible attacks on Homer's poetry (he liked to boast that he was the 'castigator' of Homer), it was Ptolemy himself who condemned him to death 'for parricide'. The Museum – including the books collected on its shelves and the men who lived among them – was Ptolemy's property and one of the instruments of his power. The accession of a new king could therefore bring far-reaching changes in the bird-cage. When

Ptolemy III Euergetes came to the throne, a new era began for Callimachus, who had written in praise of the beauty of his queen, Berenice – a native, like the poet, of Cyrene. The great sage Eratosthenes, who had close links with Callimachus, was summoned from Cyrene to the court, not only to take charge of the royal heir's education but also to direct the library. Apollonius had broken with the court, given up his position and retired to Rhodes. This did not lead to any reconciliation with Callimachus, who seized the opportunity of insulting him in a poem 'full of filth and poison'.

The learned men of the Museum were a select group; picked out and protected by the king, they enjoyed a sheltered and materially secure way of life. Even when they left the Museum they were still within the palace domains. We do not know what led Aristophanes of Byzantium, after so many years spent poring over the contents of the shelves, to organize an escape. It was said that he had hoped to travel to Pergamum, where a rival to the Museum had been emerging. But the plan was discovered, and the great scholar was arrested.

IX

The Rival Library

NELEUS'S heirs now had to guard against a graver and more immediate danger: the library of Pergamum. When Eumenes, the son of Attalus, came to the throne, he embarked on a veritable hunt for books, using methods like those the Ptolemies had employed for the last hundred years. The rivalry between the two centres had some damaging consequences. Forgers appeared in throngs, offering counterfeit antique scrolls which they had patched up from oddments or simply produced from scratch: unless these were obvious fakes, the librarians hesitated to refuse them for fear that they might be snapped up by their rivals. The scrolls were often quite sophisticated pieces of work, mixtures of the genuine and the forged on which considerable skill and effort had been bestowed.

For instance, the library at Pergamum acquired a complete collection of Demosthenes – fuller, it seemed, than the collection at Alexandria. It included one precious novelty, a new Philippic, which filled a troublesome lacuna. This was the Philippic delivered by Demosthenes before the celebrated and ill-starred battle of Chaeronea: not on the eve of battle, but only a few months earlier. It was a declaration of war, the last roar of the lion of Greek freedom before it was defeated – an exceptionally valuable acquisition, which reduced the standing of the collections hitherto current, all the more so since only twelve of Demosthenes' political speeches had been preserved. Perhaps, indeed, the true figure was not twelve but eleven, for some of Callimachus's critics had argued that the speech *On Halonnesus* had been given not by Demosthenes but by his friend and supporter Hegesippus. All in all, it was as if a new Homeric poem or Aeschylean tragedy had been discovered.

The new Pergamum edition was a great success, superseding its rivals and establishing itself as the standard text of Demosthenes. The new Philippic was accompanied, moreover, by another document, a 'Letter from Philip to the Athenians': an unusual production, admittedly, but this did not trouble the learned men of Pergamum, in ecstasies over their wonderful acquisition. Here, indeed, was further cause for rejoicing: not one, but two new texts.

The Alexandrians were not slow to react. Just as the plagiarism of the forger-poets had been unmasked by Aristophanes of Byzantium, this Philippic was exposed: someone in the Museum, recognising its phrases, consulted the library shelves and traced the original from which it had been copied. The so-called new speech of Demosthenes was to be found 'to the letter' in Book Seven of the *Historiae Philippicae* of Anaximenes of Lampsacus. However, the revelation of the forgery did not affect the success of the 'complete' Pergamum edition. Even the Alexandrians took account of this, and acquired their own copy. As late as the Augustan period, the learned men of the Museum included the pseudo-Philippic in their commentaries on Demosthenes, though they would add a preliminary note insisting on its inauthenticity. One of their number – the famous Didymus, he of the 'bronze bowels', a zealous worker but not a brilliant intellect – rather ludicrously noted that 'some people say that this speech is not authentic because it is found word for word in the *Philippicae* of Anaximenes'! It is hard to see how a known forgery could have enjoyed a more successful career.

On occasion, the scholars would themselves fabricate forgeries by way of amusement, a pastime that has flourished until a very recent date. A certain Cratippus composed a learned historical work in which he passed himself off as an Athenian, a contemporary and intimate of Thucydides. The title of this strange work, *Everything Thucydides Left Unsaid*, hinted at its character: it was full of wisdom after the event. The book was not taken seriously at Alexandria, for Cratippus, after all, made it clear that he was dealing with problems connected with Thucydides' tomb which had been posed by the archaeological discoveries of Polemon of Ilium; and he cited Zopyrus, a recent author. This gave the game away, perhaps intentionally. Didymus, who made a special study of the affair, regarded both Cratippus and Zopyrus as learned 'nonsense-mongers'. For all that, Dionysus of Halicarnassus (whose scholarship bore the stamp of Pergamum) and Plutarch after him both made use of Cratippus's work as if the author had really been what he pretended to be – a contemporary of Thucydides, familiar with the secret reasons that had led the Athenian historian to cease incorporating passages of direct speech at a certain point in his *History*.

These were not the only ways of discrediting one's rivals. Unlikely stories were invented: at Pergamum, for instance, it was put about that Ptolemy Euergetes had robbed the Athenians of the 'original' texts of the three tragedians by means of a particularly low trick. The story was incredible, for there could be no question of any 'original', the relevant text being the 'official' version prepared by the orator Lycurgus in the time of Demosthenes. Aristotle, as a student of the drama, was undoubtedly familiar with this, and given the special relationship between the Alexandrians and the Peripatetic School it must certainly have made its way to Alexandria long before Ptolemy Euergetes saw the light of day.

The conflict took on a sharper edge when the Egyptians stopped the export of papyrus. This was meant to be a rapid, if crude, way of bringing the rival library to its knees, for papyrus was the commonest and most convenient and customary writing material. The response at Pergamum was to develop and perfect the technique, of eastern origin, for treating skin to make parchment (the noun 'parchment' is derived, via medieval Latin, from the place-name 'Pergamum'). Centuries later, when the design of books altered, the new material was to gain the ascendancy. However, the struggle between the two libraries ran much deeper than this, and involved a profound difference in scholarly approach. At Pergamum, where the influence of Stoic thought prevailed, questions were asked of the classical texts, and answers quite casually given, in a manner that made the Alexandrians' hair stand on end. Textual criticism at Pergamum, based on the theory of anomalies, let the strangest readings stand: a lax enough procedure, but less damaging in terms of authenticity than the arbitrary meddling which struck out entire passages of so famous a text as Demosthenes' _On the Crown_ on the grounds that the great orator could never have used such 'vulgar' language. The Alexandrians toiled long and hard to reach what they regarded as incontrovertible conclusions, making careful lexical studies and accurate collations (Aristarchus, for instance, had concluded after much labour that the term _daita_, 'meal', in line five of the _Iliad_, could not stand since it was usually applied to the food of men rather than of beasts). Such subtleties held no attraction for the men of Pergamum, who cured all cases of textual doubt with their panacea of 'anomaly'. What interested them was the 'hidden' meaning, the meaning that lay 'behind' the classical, and especially the Homeric, texts – the 'allegory', as they called it, concealed within these poems. The Alexandrians, by contrast, patiently found line-by-line and word-by-word explanations, halting wherever the sense was not plain to them.

One hardly knows, at times, which side of the argument to take. Zenodotus, for example, calmly dismissed as inauthentic the entire passage of the _Iliad_, some 125 lines long, describing Achilles' shield: his somewhat disarming argument is that no similar passage is found anywhere else in the poem. Crates, the over-imaginative champion of the scholarship of Pergamum, took a very different view, claiming that in these lines Homer was really describing not a shield, but the ten celestial circles. All this, as can be imagined, delighted the Stoics, for it brought their teachings to a growing circle of educated people. Even so exceptional an intellect as Posidonius discussed Homer in this fashion, claiming to have discovered the theory of the tides between the lines of the *Iliad* and the *Odyssey*.

Pergamum, unlike Alexandria, could thus quite happily do without the authentic writings of Aristotle, even when it came to questions of detail. In the dispute over where the poet Alcman had been born, the experts at Pergamum rejected Sparta in favour of Sardis (as, indeed, did Aristarchus), but the fact that Aristotle also took this view left them altogether indifferent. If the kings and librarians of Pergamum were eager to acquire the relics said to belong to Neleus's heirs at Scepsis, this was chiefly for reasons of prestige: it would be pleasant to hold such treasures within one's grasp, and it would be particularly pleasant to possess a prize that had eluded the Ptolemies.

Neleus's heirs, however, were 'ignoramuses', in the doleful words of Tyrannion. Only by hiding their treasure, so they believed, would they be able to keep it safe from the hands of the royal librarians. A deep hole was dug underneath their house, and there the precious scrolls were left. Their owners gave no further thought to them: they were valuables to be hoarded, not books to be studied. It never occurred to them that damp and moths might spoil their buried treasure.

X

Reappearance and
Disappearance of Aristotle

O N his deathbed, the last sovereign of Pergamum left his kingdom to the Roman Senate and people. This led to an uprising: the Romans had great difficulty in securing their unexpected legacy, and the territory was laid waste by fire and the sword. The rebel leader, Andronicus, claimed to be an illegitimate scion of the royal house. He had chosen a very favourable moment: at Rome, the Senate had to grapple with Tiberius Gracchus, and in Sicily hundreds of thousands of slaves had risen in a rebellion which proved very difficult to contain. When eventually the storm had blown over, and the former kingdom of Pergamum had become the Roman Province of Asia, one of Neleus's descendants (we do not know which one) dug up the buried scrolls and sold them, for a large sum in gold, to a bibliophile, one Apellicon of Teos. Apellicon thus acquired a collection which the old Hellenistic rulers, with all their wealth, had been unable to obtain.

As well as a bibliophile, he prided himself on being something of a philosopher – of the peripatetic school, naturally, given his honorary Athenian citizenship (though by this time the School no longer existed in Athens). In reality, he was no more than a fanatical antiquarian who also happened to be a rather shady character: on one occasion, his mania for antiquities had led him to steal the autograph copies of some Attic decrees from the Athenian state archives, a crime for which he was lucky to escape the death penalty. But the tides of history often cause unexpected eddies in the lives of individuals. Apellicon benefited from the rise to power of the new 'tyrant' Athenion. Athenion, too, had dabbled in the ideas of the peripatetics, and Apellicon had no difficulty in winning his favour. He had botched up an edition, the first edition, of the reputedly lost texts of Aristotle, working away with steady incompetence from the scrolls that he had bought. Tyrannion, who subsequently examined this edition, pronounced it deplorable: Apellicon, who lacked any expert knowledge, had filled the gaps with inventions of his own wherever the moths had nibbled at the papyrus and obliterated the manuscript. But the project, badly executed as it was, brought Apellicon a certain renown, and in particular it impressed Athenion, who had been instructed in philosophy by the unfortunate Erymneus, last relict of the now defunct School.

Athenion's claim to citizenship was probably spurious, for his mother was said to have been a slave. However, he was a good demagogue. When Mithridates, the last great Hellenistic sovereign capable of standing his ground against the Romans, broke through the Roman defences in Asia and carried his forces into Greece, Athenion was quick to rally to his flag. He sent a stream of messages to the Athenians, assuring them that Mithridates would restore democracy and that the Romans' days as rulers of Asia were numbered. When the occasion seemed ripe, he decided to return to Athens. However, a storm cast his ship ashore in southern Euboea, near Caristus. News of the disaster spread, and a fleet left Athens to rescue the hero, whose life was thought to have been in peril. The rescue party took a litter with feet of gold, in which to bear this new Alcibiades home; and when they arrived back at Piraeus, it did seem like a reenactment of the triumphant return of Alcibiades, so often described by the historians. Posidonius, a particularly reliable witness, tells us that a mass of people thronged the quay

> to admire this paradox of fortune: here was Athenion, his citizenship obtained by deceit, borne into the city upon a gorgeous sedan chair with his feet wrapped in purple rugs – Athenion, who until that day had never worn a hint of purple, even in his cloak.

The hero's progress drew thickening crowds in its train. Everybody wanted to touch the new leader, to lay a hand on his clothes. At length they reached the portico of Attalus, and Athenion mounted the platform to address the vast crowd. He rolled his eyes, glaring in all directions; then, when complete silence had fallen all around, he fixed his eyes on his audience and began to speak.

'Athenians!' he began. 'I know that I should tell you the tidings that I bear, but I am silenced by their mighty import. . . .'

From the square in front of him, a great uproar arose: the whole crowd was calling on him to take courage, to speak out. He did not keep them waiting long.

'Very well,' he said. 'Let me announce what exceeds your wildest dreams. King Mithridates now holds dominion over the whole of Asia from Cappadocia to Cilicia. The kings of Persia and Armenia follow in his retinue like common brigands.'

Then came the most welcome news of all. 'The Roman praetor, Quintus Oppius, has surrendered. He follows in chains behind Mithridates' chariot. Manius Aquilius, the consul who massacred the slaves of Sicily, is being dragged along, on foot, under a strong guard. They have chained him up together with a big brute of a barbarian from the Danube. The Romans are panic-stricken. Some of them are disguising themselves as Greeks. Some fling themselves to the ground and beg for mercy. A few are ready to deny outright that they are Romans. And from everywhere, messengers are arriving with a single plea: Mithridates, destroy Rome!'

Here Athenion paused to allow the crowd to give vent to their enthusiasm. Only when silence had fallen once again did he bring out the question he had been holding in reserve.

'Athenians,' he asked, flattering his audience still more, 'what do I propose to do now?'

His hearers thought of Demosthenes, who had often made such appeals, and whom Athenion was imitating.

'My proposal', he continued, 'is as follows. Let our locked temples be unlocked! Let crowds fill our abandoned gymnasia and our empty theatres! How much longer shall our tribunals be silent, and the Pnyx deserted?'

He continued in this vein for some while, says Posidonius, until eventually the crowd made him their 'supreme commander', by acclamation, there and then. Gratified as he was, Athenion bore in mind the deeply rooted democratic culture of his audience: 'I accept with thanks,' he said, 'but you must realise that you will henceforth be your own commanders. I am no more than your guide. If you give me your support, my strength will be your strength.'

He then put forward a list of proposed archons, which was approved before he had even finished reading it. And yet within a few days, Posidonius observes, this follower of the peripatetics and accomplished play-actor had proclaimed himself 'tyrant', the doctrine of Aristotle and Theophrastus notwithstanding – striking confirmation, comments Posidonius, of the truth of the infallible adage that swords should never be placed in the hands of children. It was not long before the new regime's character became clear. Those whom Posidonius refers to as 'the better people' took flight, letting themselves down from the city walls, but Athenion sent the cavalry after them. Those who were not slain on the spot were brought back to Athens in chains.

The new 'tyrant' found employment for his loyal follower Apellicon, making him a counsellor and sending him to Delos. At Delos, Apellicon mismanaged things disastrously: taken by surprise by the Roman consul, he had to flee headlong, and his troops were annihilated. Meanwhile, the situation as a whole was growing critical.

Sulla had laid siege to Athens, and on 1 March, in 86 BC, he took it by storm. Turning a deaf ear to the pleas of the Athenians, who invoked the glories of their past, he decided to punish them by sacking the city. To those who remonstrated with him, he replied coldly: 'I am not here to learn ancient history.' Apellicon was among the first victims. When the legionaries broke into his house, he realised that all was lost, and prepared to meet his death among his books with the dignity appropriate to one of the last martyrs of Greek thought. His valuable library, which (so Posidonius tells us) included the works of many authors besides Aristotle, became part of Sulla's personal booty.

Years later, those few intimates of the dictator who were invited to one of his villas might enjoy the opportunity of admiring a real rarity: the old and dilapidated scrolls that had belonged to Neleus of Scepsis. Sulla's personal librarian was charged with unrolling these scrolls so that his master's visitors could examine them, and he would remain to keep an eye on them should they wish to copy a passage. However, the librarian was not above corruption, and it is well known that scholars in pursuit of books will sometimes sink to the lowest depths.

Tyrannion was living in Rome. He had arrived in the capital as a prisoner of war, but had been released. Thanks to his exceptional learning, he soon became a friend of Atticus, Cicero and their circle. He was both a serious scholar and a bibliophile (he collected a private library that ran to several thousand scrolls), and as a devotee of Aristotelian thought he was well aware that he could put these precious original manuscripts to much better use than the ill-prepared Apellicon had done. He made frequent visits to the villa, conversed with the librarian (Sulla had recently died), discussed philosophical and grammatical topics with him. In due course he made an offer, and eventually he obtained the scrolls on loan and was able to set to work on the long-cherished project of a new edition. He worked calmly and unhurriedly. It never occurred to him that the compliant librarian might already have rendered similar services to plenty of other people – in particular, to unscrupulous booksellers, who proceeded to flood the market with a torrent of copies, made by third-rate copyists. Book-collecting had become all the rage among the Roman plutocracy. 'Of what use are whole collections of books,' thundered a Stoic philosopher, 'when their owners barely find time in the course of their lives to read their titles? Devote yourself to a few books, and do not wander here and there amongst a multitude of them.'

Tyrannion lost heart and gave up. He entrusted the entire project to the distinguished logician Andronicus of Rhodes, the most illustrious living representative of the peripatetic tradition. Andronicus also took on the ungrateful task of subdividing the master's *Treatises* into books. Meanwhile, the originals had been returned to Sulla's library, which for some time had been in the possession of his son Faustus, Pompey's son-in-law. It was to Faustus's house that the cultural élite of Rome would go to consult the precious texts. We have a letter from Cicero to Atticus, in which the writer expresses his delight at being 'in Faustus's library', but then goes on to say that he is put in mind of Atticus's study, with its comfortable couch beneath the bust of Aristotle.

He would rather be sitting there, under the shadow of the Stagirite, he says, or walking with his friend in his friend's house, than seated in 'this wretched official chair' (*in istorum sella curuli*).

Faustus, however, was a megalomaniac (when Pompey had profanely invaded the temple at Jerusalem, he had wanted to be the first to break in). He was also a spendthrift, and his debts eventually obliged him to sell off everything he owned, including the library inherited from his father. So it was that the Aristotelian scrolls disappeared forever. We have no evidence that the scholars of Alexandria made any further attempt to find them. Alexandria, indeed, was preoccupied with other matters, for the country was shaken by a growing dynastic upheaval. In the letter written to Atticus from Faustus's villa, Cicero refers to rumours that the king of Egypt is about to return to the throne, and asks if they are true.

XI

The Second Visitor

A ROMAN citizen, in what must have been a moment of folly, had killed a cat in the streets of Alexandria. Then, not without a qualm of anxiety, he had gone home. Within hours, his house was surrounded. Unless he could escape (and there was no chance of that), he faced certain death: in such a case, no time would be wasted on formalities. Diodorus, who was present at the scene, saw messengers arrive from Ptolemy himself and beg the crowd to spare the Roman's life. This was unprecedented, but it was to no avail. Calm returned only when the man's unrecognisable corpse lay in the empty street.

Diodorus understood this outbreak of madness, for he had already been some while in Alexandria, and had noticed the veneration accorded to these half-wild creatures. In Sicily (Diodorus was from Agyrion) and in southern Italy, cats were beginning to appear, but they were kept apart from the domestic animals, whom they terrified. Diodorus had learned how to behave – that if by chance he came upon a cat's body in the street, he must shout, 'It was already dead!'; that he must not smile when he saw someone bowing as a cat went past; and so on. None of this puzzled him any longer. What he found incredible was the blindness of the murderous crowd: how could they have stoned a Roman citizen to death (and for such a reason!) while the Roman delegation was actually in Alexandria? For the Romans had finally condescended to negotiate with Ptolemy (popularly known as Auletes, 'the flute-player'), and to offer him official recognition and the title of 'friend and ally' of the Roman people.

For twenty years, ever since his accession, the 'flute-player' had been in danger of losing his throne. This was due to the criminal folly of his predecessor, who had found time, in his very brief reign, to attempt to profane Alexander's tomb, and then to bequeath the kingdom of Egypt to the Romans. The Alexandrians had called him 'the clandestine', but he had been well liked at Rome; taken prisoner by Mithridates, he had escaped and joined Sulla in 86 BC, and it was with Sulla that he had come to Rome. The Romans had always pretended to take his testament very seriously, for it was a means of blackmailing the 'flute-player' and squeezing money out of him, a trade successfully practised by a host of minor and not so minor functionaries (on behalf, of course, of their political masters). And now, when the Romans had at last deigned to recognise Ptolemy Auletes and to admit that the ludicrous will was of no standing, what should happen but this episode of the cat, with all its unpleasant and sadly inevitable consequences?

However, Caesar happened to be a man of his word – and Ptolemy had paid him six thousand talents to encourage him to keep it. The Alexandrians, meanwhile, were themselves losing patience with this semi-king, and they eventually drove him out. The consul Gabinius, Pompey's representative, took three years to restore him to the throne. It was at this period that Cicero asked Atticus for confirmation of the latest news.

Diodorus, a native of central Sicily, had come to Egypt to compile a historical *magnum opus*. Historians, he knew, had been divided by Polybius into two categories: those who immerse themselves in the actuality of events, drawing the material for their works from their own concrete experience (these alone, said Polybius, being worthy of esteem), and those who take an easier course, seeking out some 'city well supplied with libraries' where they can sit at their desks, consult an atlas, and travel, as Ariosto would have put it, 'with Ptolemy the geographer'. Diodorus was of the latter school. But as Polybius's ideas were much in vogue among the Greek and Roman public, it was as well to display some first-hand experience, and Diodorus accordingly fabricated a series of voyages he had never made. The philosophical proem to his work tells us that the author

> has travelled through much of Asia and Europe, undergoing all manner of hardships and dangers, in order to behold in person everything, or as nearly as possible everything, of which this history treats. We are well aware that the majority of historians, including some of the best known, have made numerous geographical errors.

These words of severe reproof were in fact taken verbatim from Polybius. His journey to Egypt was the sole voyage Diodorus had ever made.

Alexandria was an eminently sensible choice for anyone in search of a city endowed with libraries. Rome, admittedly, was much closer, but at Rome one had to curry favour with some great lord or scholar whose house was full of books: someone such as Sulla, Lucullus, Varro or Tyrannion. There were other reasons, too, why Diodorus had chosen to come to Egypt. He had become convinced of Egypt's importance. The books which had formed his mind had given the notion that history had begun there. The gods had been born there, life had originated there, and there the first observations of the stars had been made. Diodorus was an enthusiast for Stoic astrology, and the Egypt of Nechops and Petosiris, of Hermes Trismegistus, was a land he longed to see. He accordingly resolved to go there. As well as books in plenty, there would be priests in plenty, who would satisfy the curiosity of the visitor and show him the ancient annals preserved in their temples.

He was dazzled by the wealth and splendour of Alexandria: this teeming city, it seemed to him, boasted greater riches than any other metropolis. He had to visit Rome, too, once he had mastered the language, to write the Roman portion of his work. This work, universal in scope, was to fall into three parts, corresponding to Diodorus's three-fold vision of the world: Greece, Rome, Sicily. His stay in Rome, he tells us, paying the customary tribute, was long and comfortable, as was to be expected in the 'sublime' city 'which has extended its dominion to the limits of the world'.

His method of work was quite basic. He simply summed up what was to be found in already well-known books;

sometimes, indeed, for instance when he judged that his theme was already handled clearly in the source, he simply copied from them. In this way he put together forty thick scrolls – forty-two, in the event, for scrolls I and XVII proved so bulky that they had to be subdivided. He finished his work, many years later, back in Sicily, entitling it *Bibliotheca Historica,* the 'bookshelf of history', a title which earned the mocking praise of the great Pliny, who commented after Diodorus's death that it represented something of a landmark in the history of historiography. 'Among the Greeks,' wrote Pliny, 'Diodorus put an end to fabrications, frankly entitling his history *Bibliotheca.*'

He made use of standard, indeed obvious, works: Ephorus for Greek history, Megasthenes for Indian history. His needs were adequately met by the library which had grown up outside the palace, the so-called 'daughter' library, which was in fact intended for the use of scholars not attached to the Museum: as the rhetorician Aphthonius rather pompously proclaimed, it 'gave the whole city the opportunity to philosophise'. It seems to have been established as early as the reign of Ptolemy Philadelphus, and was situated in the precincts of the temple of Serapis, in the original Egyptian district of Rhakotis where the city of Alexandria had first sprung up. The 'daughter' library received duplicate copies from the Museum; in the time of Callimachus, it already contained 42,800 scrolls. Unlike the Museum, it did not collect scrolls from far and wide – scrolls in tens of thousands, from which the labour of scholars and copyists eventually extracted a quintessence of definitive texts. In the daughter library there were nothing but copies, excellent copies, of the good editions prepared in the Museum.

Diodorus never mentions the Museum, not even in his descriptions of the plan of Alexandria and of the royal palace, where (strange to say) he uses the same expressions, in the same order, as Strabo was to use – and Strabo does mention the Museum. Diodorus's favourite reading was of a type plentifully available in the Egypt of his day. He liked historical-utopian romances such as Euhemerus's *Sacred Scripture,* the 'romance' of Troy or the Amazon stories of Dionysius the 'leather-armed'. He also enjoyed the philosophico-mysterious tales of Osiris, identified syncretically with the beneficent Dionysus worshipped by the Greeks. Above all, he enjoyed Hecataeus of Adbera's *History of Egypt.* Hecataeus delighted him, and the first book of the *Bibliotheca* is based almost entirely on his writings. He reappears in the final book, Book XL, as a valuable and favourably disposed source of material on Moses and the Jewish people. Hecataeus reinforced Diodorus's conviction that the Egyptian people was of great antiquity (notwithstanding the contrary opinion expressed by Ephorus, on whom Diodorus also drew). It was from Hecataeus that Diodorus took the notion that there was a deep and substantial identity between Egyptian and Greek conceptions of justice, and that he derived the myth that the ancient Egyptians had possessed a wisdom attained only in later days by the legislators of other nations — ideas which reflected the Greek-Macedonian domination of Egypt. He found many other strange notions, too: for example, that the grandeur of an edifice was strictly related to the number of its inhabitants, from which he concluded that Moses, who had promoted that demographic increase of his people, was the model of a good political strategist.

Diodorus also visited Thebes. Following the directions in Hecataeus's book, he travelled as far as the valley of the royal tombs, noting however that 'at the time when we arrived in these places' even the surviving tombs seen by Hecataeus 'had largely fallen into ruin'. Rameses' mausoleum was still there, and Diodorus decided to describe it. Being unable to get access to it, he contented himself with giving a very faithful report of Hecataeus's description, which he copied out assiduously without worrying about its strange and obscure aspects. The description of Rameses' tomb is the only point at which Diodorus explicitly mentions Hecataeus's name, even though his book on Egypt is everywhere indebted to him. Perhaps we should see this as a sign of the importance which Hecataeus himself had been anxious to ascribe to his visit to Thebes, and in particular to the plan of the mausoleum.

XII

War

T OWARDS nightfall, a small boat had come alongside the palace wall, unseen by anyone. A little later a man, apparently a carpet-seller, had asked to be shown into Caesar's presence. He said that he was called Apollodorus, and came from Sicily. Once admitted, he unrolled his bundle under the amused gaze of the Roman general. From it emerged Cleopatra, who had concealed herself in a linen bag of the kind used to carry carpets. Plutarch tells us that when the bag was opened to reveal Cleopatra stretched at full length (not that she was very tall), Caesar was enchanted by the lady's impudence. She for her part showed no trace of embarrassment, and at once engaged him in a beguiling conversation in Greek.

Although he was Ptolemy's guest, Caesar readily agreed to mediate in the dispute between the king and his sister Cleopatra, son and daughter of the 'flute-player' who had been of such assistance to him in the early stages of his difficult career. Caesar did not feel altogether at ease – Pompey had met his end not long since – but he accepted the suggestion that a splendid banquet should be given to celebrate the successful outcome of the negotiations. All

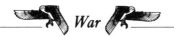

was not quiet in the vast palace during the festivities. Ptolemy's powerful general, Achillas, architect of Pompey's downfall, was conspiring in a remote room with the eunuch Pothinus, the king's treacherous tutor. Taking advantage of the confusion and excitement of the banquet, they were planning to do away with Caesar too. But Caesar's barber, the most loyal of slaves and the most timorous of men, sensed that something was amiss. All the feasting laid on to dull the senses of the guests failed to put him off his guard. He began to creep along corridors and in and out of rooms, eavesdropping, and at length he found himself outside the door behind which Achillas was closeted with Pothinus. At once he grasped what was going on, and ran to warn Caesar. Caesar had that wing of the palace surrounded, hoping to surprise the two men in the act of treachery. Pothinus was captured and killed, but Achillas made good his escape. Once outside, he organized an uprising of the Alexandrians against the guest trapped with his few armed men in the palace.

Never, perhaps, had Caesar found himself in a situation so unpromising from a strategic point of view. Lucan, in his poem on the civil war, tells us that Caesar,

> placing no trust in the city walls, barricaded himself behind the palace gateways, like a noble beast trembling in a narrow cage, breaking its teeth as it gnaws savagely at the bars. . . . The bold spirit which not long before, in Thessaly, had looked without fear on the army of the Senate and on Pompey now trembled at a slaves' plot, and cowered in a palace beneath showers of arrows.

In the event, Achillas actually first attempted to force the surrender of the palace by cutting off the water conduits. He then tried to mount an attack in force from the sea. His army was irregular enough, but it had a large complement of Roman deserters, who had been in Egypt since the time of Gabinius and who fought like lions to preserve the country's status as an independent zone where they could continue to find shelter. Caesar successfully countered this attack, despite his lack of troops: 'although besieged,' writes Lucan, 'he fought like a besieger'. Caesar's men then set fire to the sixty ships of Ptolemy's fleet riding at anchor in the port. The fire spread to other areas of the city, and the besieging force, obliged to turn its attention to the march of the flames, slackened its grip on the palace.

Our only account of the fire's spread comes from Lucan. He tells us that Caesar, besieged in the palace, 'ordered that torches soaked with pitch should be thrown on the ships that stood ready to attack'. One wall of the palace directly overlooked the sea (it was against this wall that Achillas's ships had launched their unsuccessful assault), and it was presumably from this wing that the pitch-soaked torches were flung. 'The fire soon blazed up,' Lucan continues, 'for it spread to the rigging and to the decks, which oozed resin.' Devoured by flames, the first ships began to sink, and meanwhile 'the fire spread beyond the ships. The houses nearest to the waterside caught fire too.' The wind 'hastened the calamity: the flames were driven by the gusts and ran like meteors along the rooftops. . . . The disaster drew most of the besieging force away from the palace to defend the city.' Taking advantage of this respite, Caesar moved his quarters to Pharos. Here, controlling the maritime access

route into the city, he could await the reinforcements he badly needed.

The fire, then, distracted the besieging force as it developed at some distance from the palace. The first and most serious damage was obviously suffered by the area around the port: shipyards, arsenals, and the warehouses and depots in which 'grain and books' were stored. These buildings, immediately adjacent to the harbour installations, contained 'by chance', at the time of the fire, some forty thousand book scrolls of excellent quality. We owe these two pieces of information respectively to Dion Cassius and to Orosius, both of whom drew their material from Livy (as, for the matter of that, did Lucan). Caesar, on the other hand, in his own account of the early stages of the Alexandrian war, says nothing about the destruction of

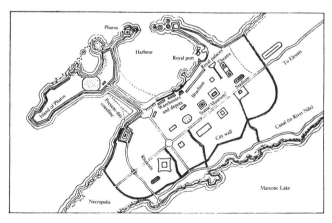

2. *Plan of Alexandria in Ptolemaic times (Gustav Parthey's reconstruction).*

any goods (grain or books) stored in the port warehouses, although he records the fact that the ships were set alight and dwells on its strategic significance. Indeed, one of his lieutenants, who wrote a continuation of the *Commentaries* after Caesar's death, praises the building materials used at Alexandria, saying that they proved resistant to the fire.

Since the treasures of the Museum cannot possibly have been outside the palace walls, let alone stored in the port alongside the grain depots, we need hardly stress that the scrolls which went up in flames were quite unconnected with the royal library. Had Orosius been referring to scrolls from the Museum, he would scarcely have spoken, paraphrasing Livy, of books found there 'by chance'. The books must accordingly have been articles of merchandise, export goods intended for the valuable and fastidious foreign market. They must have been on their way to Rome or to one of the other cultured cities whose needs were supplied by the industrious Alexandrian booksellers, whom Tyrannion disparaged as he did their Roman counterparts.

XIII

The Third Visitor

T HE royal library thus remained unscathed by this first
outbreak of conflict in the streets of the Ptolemaic
capital. There was no 'sack of Alexandria', for Caesar and
his long-awaited reinforcements won their decisive victory
outside the city walls. Ptolemy was routed and drowned in
the Nile, and Caesar put Cleopatra on the throne as joint
ruler with her official husband, Ptolemy XIV. Her true
prince consort was Caesar himself. Cleopatra was shrewd
enough to present him with a son (she persuaded him, at
all events, that the child was his), whom the Alexandrians
playfully called 'Caesarion' (*Kaisarion*).

Caesar's marked taste for playing the king in Egypt,
since he could not openly play the king at Rome, of
course alarmed not only his long-standing enemies but
also some of his own followers. The Roman senators
and *equites* regarded the rest of the world simply as an
udder to be milked dry, and for them Caesar's fancy for
Cleopatra was just a tiresome episode: but if we see things
in a less narrow perspective we must acknowledge that
Egypt under the queen had acquired greater importance
and prestige than it had enjoyed for centuries. For this

reason Cleopatra was obliged, a few years later, to take pains to beguile Mark Antony just as she had beguiled the now vanquished Caesar. Antony, a far less intellectually complex and demanding figure than his great predecessor, set about impressing the queen: his detractors reported that he had decided to present her, among other gifts, with two hundred thousand scrolls from the library at Pergamum. This calumny – for there was no truth in the story – was perhaps intended as a gibe at Antony's ignorance of literary matters. Imagine giving books (which belonged, properly speaking, to the State of Rome) to the woman who owned the world's greatest and most famous library!

Following the defeat of Cleopatra – a defeat which resulted from her willingness to run risks: Horace makes the point in frank and far from conventional poetry – Egypt was given special constitutional status, under the direct control of Octavian. Octavian, the chief of the triumvirs and the restorer of the *res publica*, wanted to make sure that in future nobody would be able to make the palace of Alexandria into a personal power base. It was said that Caesar had feared the same danger, and would have preferred to make Egypt a protectorate of his own rather than a province of the Empire. Subsequent events vindicated his anxiety. The first prefect of Egypt, Cornelius Gallus, who defeated Antony in the final skirmish outside Alexandria, had no sooner taken up his post than he began to cover the province's pyramids and obelisks with trilingual inscriptions praising his own exploits. He even planned to erect a huge inscription in the walls of the sacred island of Elephantina, in the first cataract on the Nile, a place of symbolic importance where the Pharaohs used to assemble their armies at the start of their campaigns. Cornelius Gallus, clearly, must be persuaded to put an end to himself. . . . In 26 BC, he did so.

The following year, Strabo the Stoic came to Egypt in the retinue of the new prefect, Aelius Gallus. He was to remain there almost five years. Strabo was an exceptional figure, whose recently published *Continuation of Polybius* had already won him a scholarly reputation. He came from Amasia, in Pontus, the birthplace of Mithridates (with whom he had long-standing family connections), and had been a student since his earliest years, first in Alexandria under Xenarchus, the Peripatetic, and then at Rome, where he had been one of Tyrannion's circle – and had heard the complicated saga of the Aristotelian texts. Now, as befitted a Stoic, he was preparing to complement history with geography. He made Egypt the starting-point for his projected geographical *magnum opus*, though in the actual work the country is described not first (as in Diodorus) but last. He was still in Alexandria in the year 20, when an Indian delegation passed through the city. Their baggage ncluded an enormous snake, a gift for Augustus, then in Samos. Strabo made a point of including this episode in his *Geography*.

While at work in the Museum library, where he was able to consult works unobtainable elsewhere, Strabo studied the complicated problem of the flow of the Nile, which had baffled Greek science since the days of Thales and Herodotus and which Diodorus had dealt with simply by transcribing a few chapters from Agatharchides of Cnidus.

The library of Alexandria was certainly not the epicentre of world learning and science any longer, but it was enjoying something of a renaissance now that the monarchy had come to an end and the storms of dynastic rivalry had finally subsided. In their way, the voluminous works of Didymus are evidence of this revival. A native and inhabitant of Alexandria, Didymus had never felt impelled to visit Rome, and he knew almost nothing of the school of Pergamum. Alexandria, and its 'great library' (as it was still called), provided him with all the abundant scholarly materials he needed to prepare and compile his commentaries – amounting, so Seneca informs us, to some four thousand scrolls. He dealt with authors as diverse as Homer and Demosthenes, and commented on lyrical poets, dramatists, historians, orators. His prolix commentaries in fact amounted to summaries of many authors' works, and in compiling them the indefatigable Didymus believed, with some justice, that he was carrying out his task of exegesis.

Among the near contemporaries of Didymus were Tryphon, Habron and Theon. The last-named did not confine himself to the classics, but commented on modern authors too (Callimachus, Lycophron, Theocritus, Apollonius of Rhodes, and others), and one can see that material of this kind threatened to swell the library's dimensions beyond all measure. Didymus's son, Apion, followed his father's scholarly trade, and enjoyed the esteem of no less a personage than the emperor Tiberius, who called him 'the cymbal of the world', intending to imply that his fame resounded everywhere. As well as writing an

Egyptian History in the style of Hecataeus and Manetho, Apion penned a virulent attack *Against the Jews*, reflecting the growing mood of anti-semitism which Philo deplored and which was to lead to the eventual destruction of the Jewish quarter.

Under the new form of government, the library was no longer the private possession of the reigning family. It was a public institution of the Roman province (the 'priest of the Museum' was now appointed directly by Augustus), and even seems to have been publicly described in a work *On the Museum of Alexandria* written by one of Didymus's rivals, Aristonicus of Alexandria, whom Strabo had known in Rome.

Strabo's account of Alexandria includes a precise description of the Museum:

> The Museum, too, is part of the royal palace. It comprises the covered walk, the exedra or portico, and a great hall in which the learned members of the Museum take their meals in common. Money, too, is held in common in this community; they also have a priest who is head of the Museum, formerly appointed by the sovereigns and now appointed by Augustus.

Strabo goes on to mention and describe the 'so-called *Soma*': a circular enclosure, chosen by Ptolemy I for the site of Alexander's tomb, which had subsequently come to hold the tombs of the various succeeding Ptolemies as well. 'The so-called *Soma* ("the body") is also part of the royal palace,' writes Strabo. 'It is a circular enclosure, in which the tombs of the kings and of Alexander are situated.' It seems clear that Strabo thought of the *Soma* as contiguous with the Museum. He has a good deal to say on this subject, explaining how Ptolemy first obtained possession of Alexander's body and how he gave it burial in Alexandria. It is still in Alexandria, he says (though without stating its exact location) – not in its original golden sarcophagus, but in an alabaster one, as a result of the attempt made by Ptolemy 'the clandestine' to profane the tomb.

Strabo does not mention the library, for the simple reason that it did not constitute a separate room or building.

XIV

The Library

THE key to the riddle is in the tomb of Rameses
II. Modern excavators have found no library there,
either: but Hecataeus is not a false witness, he has simply
been misunderstood. His account exists only in the later
compilation made by Diodorus, but even in this form its
phraseology is revealing. After the library, we are told,
'there followed images of all the Egyptian divinities'. How,
though, can a room 'follow' and 'be followed by' bas-reliefs,
as Hecataeus appears to state? *Bibliotheke,* which we have
hitherto rendered as 'library' (the usual translation), must
here have its original meaning of a 'shelf', a shelf on whose
surface scrolls are placed. The term, obviously, then refers
to the collection of scrolls; only by extension does it come to
denote also the room (when such rooms begin to be built) in
which the bookshelves, *bibliothekai,* are placed. The 'sacred
library' of the mausoleum was thus not a library but a shelf,
or several shelves, running along one side of the covered
walk.

It was found, to be precise, between the bas-relief showing the king offering the gods the produce of his mines and
the images of the Egyptian gods. Just as an inscription at

the bottom of the first relief showed the money value of the king's offering, so an inscription above the *bibliotheke* read: 'The place of the cure of the soul'.

Now we can also make sense of what Hecataeus tells us about the sumptuous room with the triclinia or couches. This room, which is circular, is said to have shared a common wall with the library at one point. It seems odd that the detail should be mentioned, since passage from one part of the mausoleum to another must inevitably have been by way of common walls between contiguous rooms. Once we have understood what Hecataeus means by *bibliotheke*, however, we grasp why the detail (not given on other occasions) should be drawn to our attention here: the sumptuous hall and the covered walk shared a common wall *at the point where the bookshelf ran along it*.

Let us recapitulate. The covered walk in the mausoleum of Rameses gave access to numerous rooms or chambers, adorned with pictures of all kinds of choice food. As one advanced, one encountered the bas-reliefs showing the king offering up the produce of his mines; then came the *bibliotheke;* then the images of the Egyptian gods and of the king doing homage to Osiris. Finally, in the sumptuous hall that adjoined the covered walk at the point where the bookshelf ran along its walls, the body of the sovereign was buried: a somewhat anomalous last resting-place.

The pharaoh's mysterious words ('whoever wishes to know ... where I am to be found'), which the priests translated for Hecataeus, thus defied the visitor to discover the way into the hall containing the sarcophagus. Access, we can infer, was by a passage opened in the dividing wall which Diodorus calls the 'wall in common'. The visitor was challenged not to surpass the warlike *exploits* of the pharaoh, but to surmount the difficulties posed by his complex *building* (*ergon*, 'work', can have the latter sense: see the first line of Herodotus's *Proem*) – challenged to find his bearings and discover its secrets. And because the sarcophagus was situated so high up, on the roof of the hall, the pharaoh spoke not only of *where* he could be found, but of how 'great', or how *high*, he was.

In the Museum, too, a covered walk and a room for communal meals were integral parts of the building. The *Soma* of Alexander was to be found within the Museum precincts, just as the *Soma* of Rameses was to be found within the hall in the Mausoleum. The two buildings, it is clear, were identical.

It was not a matter of chance, then, that Hecataeus devoted so much attention to Rameses' mausoleum. His account is more than a description, for there are a number of references to the later realities of the Ptolemaic period in which he lived. We are told, for instance, that the king was shown fighting 'in Bactria', and here the pharaoh – who never fought in Bactria, and who appears in the bas-relief as the victor of the battle of Kadesh, in Syria – seems suddenly identified with the Ptolemaic kings (who claimed dominion as far afield as Bactria and the Indus) or even with Alexander himself. The priests' references to 'unparalleled bravery' mixed with an ignoble 'greed for praise' are applicable to Alexander, too. Also noteworthy is the distinction drawn between Egyptian and other divinities, a distinction which could have had no meaning in an Egyptian mausoleum of the thirteenth century BC. Syncretism of this kind, symbolised in the generic 'divinity' to whom the king offers the produce of his mines, is to be attributed, rather, to the new Greek rulers of Egypt. At all events, Hecataeus's description of Rameses' mausoleum helps us to fill out Strabo's rather condensed topography of the Alexandrian Museum. For example, the rooms that gave off the large circular hall in the mausoleum must have had their counterpart in the layout of the Museum; they would have been the living quarters of its 'members'.

Hecataeus's exploration of the pharaoh's tomb was almost a voyage of initiation. Beginning beneath the starry sky of the first peristyle, he made his way through a host of images and symbols until he reached the teasing inscription at the foot of the pharaoh's colossal statue. Here, at the climax of his journey, the priests revealed the hidden meaning of the words and disclosed the whereabouts of the sarcophagus. Hecataeus, an intimate companion of Ptolemy, may have been seeking, when he described his exploration, to reveal or suggest the source of the plan on which the 'forbidden city' had been built – just as Aristeas thought he had revealed the ineffable character of the books of the Jewish law.

XV

The Fire

STRABO'S account of the plan of the Museum at Alexandria thus lacks nothing. Here, as in Rameses' 'sacred library', the shelves (*bibliothekai*) were evidently arranged along the covered walk, in the recesses that gave off it.

The same conclusion follows if we consider the plan of the library at Pergamum, unquestionably modelled on the Alexandrian Museum. Here again, the 'library' did not consist of a separate room. And in the 'daughter' library in the Serapeum at Alexandria, the books were arranged on shelves beneath the porticoes, where (Aphthonius explains) 'those who loved reading' were able to consult them freely.

The covered walk was not a mere alleyway, but a broad roofed passage. Every niche or recess must have been devoted to a particular class of authors, each distinguished by an appropriate heading (of the type used by Callimachus in his *Catalogues*). In the course of time collections of scrolls must have been stored elsewhere too, the necessary space being made available in the precincts of the Museum's two chief buildings.

Any fire which destroyed the scrolls would therefore

have reduced the two buildings to ashes. There is no record whatever of any such catastrophe. Strabo visited the buildings, worked in them and described them barely twenty years after Caesar's Alexandrian campaign.

The Dialogue of John Philoponus with the Emir Amrou Ibn el-Ass while Amrou prepared to burn the Library

HAVING raised the flag of Mohammed above the walls of Alexandria, Amrou Ibn el-Ass wrote to the caliph Omar. 'I have conquered the great city of the west,' he began,

> and I find it difficult to list its riches and its beauties. Let me say only that it contains four thousand palaces, four thousand public baths, four hundred theatres or places of amusement and twelve thousand fruit shops; and that forty thousand Jews pay tribute there. The city was conquered by force of arms and without parleying. The Moslems look forward impatiently to enjoying the fruits of their victory.

The date was the Friday of the new moon of Moharram, in the twentieth year of the *hejira* – in the Christian calendar, 22 December, 640. The emperor Heraclius was in Constantinople. Only a few years before, he had had to recapture Alexandria from the Persians, and now, his health failing, he gave orders for a desperate series of counter-attacks in the hope of retaking the metropolis. The chronicler Theophanes tells us that he died of dropsy a few weeks later in February 641. Twice the Byzantine generals fought their way to the gates of Alexandria, and twice Amrou drove them back again. The caliph rejected all talk of destroying and sacking the city, but Amrou, infuriated by the enemy's repeated attacks, made good his threat that he would lay Alexandria 'as open on every side as the dwelling of a harlot'. He had its towers pulled down and ordered much of the city wall to be destroyed. However, he restrained his men when they seemed bent on pillage, and on the spot where his words had calmed their fury he erected the mosque of Mercy.

Amrou was no unlettered warrior. Four years earlier, when occupying Syria, he had summoned the Patriarch and asked him a series of subtle and sometimes embarrassing questions concerning the holy scriptures and the supposed divinity of Christ. He had even gone to the length of asking to consult the Hebrew original, to check the accuracy of the Greek translation of a passage from Genesis that the Patriarch had cited in support of his opinions.

According to Ibn al-Kifti's _History of Wise Men_ (though some have doubted his testimony), John Philoponus was still alive, much advanced in years, when Amrou occupied Alexandria. John was a commentator on Aristotle, as indefatigable as his fine epithet ('lover of labour') implied. He was a Christian, one of the Christian fraternity of the 'Philoponi', but his Aristotelianism made him extremely prone to heresy. In his treastise _On Henosis_ he had claimed that the three Persons of the Trinity shared a single common nature, even though (he said) this was in a triple hypostasis: beneath its Aristotelian terminology, the argument had a Monophysite cast apparent to the least sophisticated reader. John found himself cornered, so to speak, when he was led to maintain that Christ's nature was solely and exclusively divine. For many years he lived the solitary life of a heretic, pursuing his grammatical and mathematical studies and his unceasing commentaries on Aristotle.

Amrou took to visiting this old man, whose arguments against the incredible confusions of the Christian doctrine of the Trinity greatly delighted him. Here was an opportunity to continue the closely-reasoned conversation he had enjoyed with the Patriarch – and this time, he felt, his interlocutor was almost of his own mind. Amrou must have been fascinated, or perhaps amused, by Christological dispute, to judge from the question he had put to the Patriarch: Did Christ, who (so the Christians claimed) was also God, govern the world, as one would expect of a god, even when he was in Mary's womb? Forced onto the defensive, the venerable Syrian had given rather a weak answer, remarking that God himself (God the Father) had not lost his power to control events even when immersed in his famous conversation with Moses, which had lasted forty days and forty nights. (As a Moslem, Amrou could not doubt the authenticity of this conversation, for it was recorded in the Pentateuch, which he too regarded as holy scripture.) Then the Patriarch had been obliged to admit that nowhere in the Pentateuch is there even a passing reference to the Trinity. He had attempted to explain the embarrassing silence of this supreme repository of truth by arguing that it would have been imprudent to discuss the topic at a time when people were still all too childishly prone to polytheism – a double-edged argument, for it involved the rash admission that to believe in the Trinity was to risk falling into polytheistic snares.

Amrou, guided by the Prophet's teaching, of course ran no danger of entanglement in such extravagances. 'God has no children,' he said. 'If he had a son, I would be the first to worship him. . . . Do not tell me there is a Trinity in God: He is one,' he would insist, and more in the same vein. Nonetheless, we can well imagine how John's arguments must have pleased him, particularly because they came (so to speak) from the enemy camp. Amrou was captivated, too, by John's strict logic, and before long they had become inseparable.

At length, John found the courage to bring up a subject which he had often meant but never dared to broach in his daily conversations with Amrou. 'You have sealed up every warehouse in Alexandria,' he began, 'and you rightly lay claim to all the goods in the city. To this I do not object. But there are certain things which are of use neither to you nor to your men, and I would like to ask you to leave them here.'

Amrou asked him what he meant.

'The books in the royal treasury,' replied John. 'You have taken possession of them, but I know that you would not know how to make use of them.'

Amrou asked in surprise who had collected these books, and John began to tell him the history of the library.

What were the books of Alexandria at this time, and where were they kept? Thirty-five years earlier, Queen Zenobia, an Arab from Palmyra who claimed descent from Cleopatra, had captured the city only to lose it again to the Emperor Aurelian. In the course of Aurelian's campaign, the Bruchion district was very seriously damaged: Ammianus tells us, though his account may exaggerate, that it was totally destroyed. A few years later, the city was completely sacked by Diocletian. The Museum, which had enjoyed periods of renewed splendour during early Imperial times and which had recently been restored once more to its old glory thanks to the notable efforts of the mathematician Diophantus, must have suffered terrible damage. The Serapeum had been destroyed in the attack on the pagan temples in 391. The last famous figure associated with the Museum had been Theon, father of the celebrated Hypatia who studied geometry and musicology and whom the Christians, convinced in their ignorance that she was a heretic, barbarously murdered in 415. In more recent times, the Persians under Chosroes had occupied the city for ten years, until Heraclius drove them out after a long and difficult struggle. Naturally, the city's books had changed, too; and not only in their content. The delicate scrolls of old had gone. Their last remnants had been cast out as refuse or buried in the sand, and they had been replaced by more substantial parchment, elegantly made and bound into thick codices – and crawling with errors, for Greek was increasingly a forgotten language. The texts now consisted chiefly of patristic writings, Acts of Councils, and 'sacred literature' in general.

But John, carried away by his theme, forgot the depredations of time, appealing to Amrou as if the books whose fate they were discussing had been the original volumes first collected by Ptolemy a thousand years ago.

'You must understand', he said, 'that when Ptolemy Philadelphus succeeded to the throne he became a seeker after knowledge and a man of some learning. He searched for books regardless of expense, offering booksellers the very best terms to persuade them to bring their wares here. He achieved his objective: before long' – here John chose a figure that would not seem too exaggerated to Amrou – 'some fifty-four thousand books were acquired.'

John then bethought himself of a text which had enjoyed great popularity with Greek writers: Aristeas' narrative, copied, summarised and rearranged time and again by Jews and Christians alike. Using it and embellishing it in his turn, John went on with his story: 'When the king was given this figure, he asked Demetrius' (Ibn al-Kifti, reporting John's words, always calls Demetrius 'Zamira') 'whether in his belief there were still any books in the world not yet obtained for the library.

'Demetrius replied that there were many: in India, in Persia, in Georgia and Armenia, in Babylon, and in many other places besides. The king, amazed at this answer, told Demetrius: "Then you must continue to seek them out." And until he died, this was always Ptolemy's policy.' (In this Arabic reworking, the world is a much larger place and the goal of collecting all its books a much more distant one than in Aristeas' original account.)

'And these books', concluded John, 'continued to be

preserved and looked after by the sovereigns and those who succeeded them right down to our own times.'

Amrou realised that his friend's narrative, and his request, were of great importance. He was silent for a moment before replying. 'In the matter of these books', he said, 'I cannot act without the permission of Omar. However, I can write to him and tell him of the extraordinary things that you have related.'

So Amrou wrote to the Caliph. On average, a letter might take twelve days on the sea voyage from Alexandria to Constantinople, and rather more than twelve days to reach Mesopotamia by land. The return journey would take a similar period. For something like a month, then, the fate of the library would remain in the balance while not only John but also the emir waited in trepidation for Omar's reply to reach them.

During these days of expectancy, John obtained Amrou's consent to visit the library with his inseparable companion Philaretes, a Jewish medical doctor and former pupil of John's who had written a work on _Pulsations_ once generally misattributed to John himself. This, John knew, might be his last farewell to the library, a farewell made all the more melancholy by the state of the long-abandoned building, whose entrance was guarded by a group of armed men. John made his way between the shelves and felt in silence the parchments that he was no longer capable of reading. Using his sense of touch, which had gradually come to supplement his failing sight, he located a manuscript and handed it to Philaretes, asking him to read the final chapter aloud. The book was Theodorus of Mopsuestia's

Explanation of the Creation, and many years before John had taken issue with it in the seven closely argued books of his *Cosmogony*, a treatise also known in the Latin world under the title *De opificio mundi*. He took pleasure in thinking through his old objections to Theodorus, and felt convinced that he had been right to maintain (as he still maintained) that natural science could be reconciled with the Biblical account of the Creation. At length, feeling rather calmer, he asked to return home.

When he arrived there, he found Amrou waiting for him. The emir had been there for some while, impatient to ask John the question that had been forming in his mind for several days. He had no wish to give unnecessary offence, and began by making conversation about the visit which he knew John had paid to the library that morning. Then he came to the point.

'When you explained about the books,' he said, 'you told me that they had always been kept the whole time among the treasures of the royal palace, from the far-off days of king Ptolemy down to our own times. However, a Greek official, a man who has become a loyal adherent of our cause, has told me in great confidence that this is not the case. He declares, on the contrary, that the whole treasury of ancient books which you told me about was burned in the great fire of Alexandria, started by the first of the Roman emperors many centuries before the birth of the Prophet. He says, too, that the half-burned shelves that survived this terrible fire are still to be seen in some of the temples in the city.'

Here, noting the agitation of his two listeners, Amrou ceased. It was plain enough, in any case, what he would have said had he continued: that John had stooped to what could only be called deceit, trying to persuade him to spare books that did not really possess the especial value claimed for them.

There was a brief silence, painful to all three men, before John asked if they could go out together. He requested Philaretes to take them to the temple of Serapis, or rather to what remained of it. John's old body seemed charged with unaccustomed energy as he prepared for this last battle, unexpected but (it now almost seemed) unconsciously desired. They were making their way towards what had once been the heart of the Egyptian quarter of Rhakotis. It was here that the followers of Christ, led by the patriarch Theophilus, had stormed the temple of Serapis, second in splendour (Ammianus had written) only to the Campidoglio at Rome. The marble, alabaster and priceless ivory of its furnishings had been smashed in fragments, and the parchment of its books had burned splendidly. Now, the site lay lost in the silence of many years: the surrounding district had never recovered from the outburst of destruction. Philaretes, immediately understanding what John had in mind, led the group towards the *armaria librorum*, the chests for storing books. He was the first to speak. He knew Latin, and had read a number of Latin books during his time at Vivarium, in Calabria, where he had worked in the library founded by Cassiodorus (a more hospitable environment, for a Jew, than Seville, the other centre of learning in the west: though Philaretes would have liked to visit the Spanish city, where Isidore, author of the *Contra Iudaeos,* held the bishopric).

'These shelves', he said, quoting a passage from Paulus Orosius, 'were emptied by men of our own times: *exinanita a nostris hominibus nostris temporibus.*'

In the detailed account which he proceeded to give, Philaretes did his best to make everything clear to Amrou. Orosius, he explained, a Portuguese historian and devoted follower of St Augustine, had in fact referred to his visit to the temple of Serapis, where he had been struck by the sight of these pitiful remnants of the bookshelves, in the course of a digression in his account of Julius Caesar's Alexandrian war. He made it clear beyond a doubt that the traces had not been left by Caesar's fire: first of all because they derived from much more recent events (still a vivid memory, in Orosius's time, for those who had witnessed them), and secondly because the Serapeum was by no means to be confused with the royal palace, where the precious Ptolemaic collections were kept. Philaretes explained that Orosius was intent on correcting a crass blunder made by Ammianus, an obscure and presumptuous Syriac writer, whose native tongue was Greek but who had chosen to write his histories in an elaborate and pretentious Latin. Ammianus had copied down his sources without understanding them, with the result that he had made Julius Caesar the author both of the sack of Alexandria and of the destruction of the Serapeum.

Amrou was impressed by the Jew's clear and concrete explanation, so different from the innuendoes and inconsistencies his earlier informant had regaled him with.

Philaretes, meanwhile, went into greater detail: it was not often that he had an opportunity to display his learning, and now that he had started he found it hard to stop. During his travels in the west, he said, he had seen more than one manuscript of Orosius's *History*. He had noticed that in the passage concerning the books stored by chance near the port (*proximis forte aedibus condita*) and destroyed when Caesar set fire to the ships, some codices put their number at forty thousand and others at four hundred thousand. There was a similar discrepancy in Aulus Gellius's *Attic Nights*, where the episode featured in a short and somewhat fanciful chapter devoted to the libraries of antiquity: some texts gave a figure of seventy thousand, others of seven hundred thousand. Warming to his theme, and forgetting that Amrou was hardly familiar with the materials on which his exposition was based, Philaretes drew his listeners' attention to what he called the definitive proof. Orosius, he said, had simply reproduced the unquestionably authentic account given by the historian Livy, who was a contemporary of Caesar and of Augustus. Livy's works in their entirety ran to almost one hundred and fifty scrolls. It was only necessary to find the book dealing with the Alexandrian war, and Livy's text would at once make it clear whether Orosius had written forty or four hundred thousand. However – this was the crux – the book in question seemed lost beyond recovery (it was possible that nobody any longer possessed a complete Livy).

But one day, Philaretes continued, he had suddenly come across a solution to the problem. He had been reading Seneca's *On the tranquillity of the soul*, and had come upon the passage in which the Stoic, whose wisdom so often borders on folly, attacks the fashionable taste that led so many rich people to fill their houses with thousands of books, collected for the sake of mere ostentation. Philaretes had found enlightenment in the following sentences:

> Of what use are books without number and complete collections if their owner barely finds time in the course of his life even to read their titles? At Alexandria, *forty thousand* books were burned. There are those who praise this as splendid testimony to the wealth of the royal house (*pulcherrimum regiae opulentiae monumentum*), and even Livy speaks in these terms, for he says that these scrolls were the fruit of the sovereigns' rare taste and painstaking care (*qui elegantiae regum curaeque egregium id opus ait fuisse*).

On the contrary, protests Seneca, they bespoke neither taste nor care, but vulgar cultural ostentation, which did not even deserve the epithet 'cultural' since the books had been acquired 'not for study but for display'. Now Orosius, concluded the triumphant Philaretes, had read and paraphrased the very passage in Livy which Seneca attacks, for he uses the same terms to describe the scrolls: '*singulare profecto monumentum studii curaeque maiorum*'. It follows that Orosius, like Seneca, must have found the figure of forty thousand scrolls, *quadraginta milia librorum*, in his copy of Livy.

But Amrou had stopped following this intricate and impassioned chain of reasoning. John indicated to Philaretes that he had perhaps said enough for the moment, and the three men returned home without any further discussion of the fascinating topic.

Days passed, and still Omar's reply did not arrive. Amrou continued to visit his two learned friends as regularly as before, but it seemed to them that his old spontaneous affability had gone, for all the efforts he made to appear cordial. A shadow had fallen between them. At length, John determined to lift this shadow if he could.

'It seems to me', he said, 'that you are not fully convinced by my dear friend Philaretes' explanation. Will you allow me to return to a theme which, as you must have realised, is dearer to us than life itself?'

Amrou readily admitted that John had, as people say, read his mind. His doubts, he said frankly, arose from the fact that Philaretes, in his complicated exposition, had acknowledged that during the Alexandrian war Caesar had indeed caused the destruction of forty thousand books.

'We, too, have often wondered what books those might have been,' replied John. 'Regrettably, most of our historians are silent on the question. Even Appianus, for instance, though he was born and lived here in Alexandria during the happy days of Emperor Hadrian, says not a word about any fire in the Museum when he discusses the Alexandrian war in his _Civil Wars_. The same goes for Athenaeus, though he was an Egyptian too, and his books are as erudite as they are interminable: he draws on thousands of sources (and even makes use of Ptolemy Physkon's writings about the royal palace of Alexandria). Our only precise detail comes from Dion Cassius, who in his own day heard Caracalla's crazy threats to burn down the Museum in revenge for the death of Alexander the Great, whom Caracalla believed to have been poisoned by Aristotle. Dion Cassius tells us that the fire destroyed the arsenal and the depots of grain and books.'

'And this', Philaretes broke in, 'tallies exactly with Orosius's account, of which I have told you. Orosius says that the burned books chanced to be in the buildings near the port – *proximis forte aedibus condita*.' He quoted the Latin phrase as if to do so might strengthen the force of his argument, and then proceeded to draw his inference. 'These buildings close to the port, then, must have been the depots mentioned by Dion!'

Amrou said that, while he was impressed by these additional details, the question he had raised still remained unanswered.

'In that case,' replied Philaretes, 'I can only conclude that you did not follow my argument through to the end when we were visiting the ruins of the Serapeum.'

Philaretes' pedantic tone rather irritated Amrou, but he was careful to show no sign of annoyance. It was really his own fault, he reflected, that they were discussing all this again.

'I said then', continued Philaretes, 'that the best record of Livy's narrative (a narrative, I repeat, that would resolve all our uncertainties if a copy were in being and if we could consult it) is found in Seneca's treatise *De Tranquillitate animi*. You will, I hope, have realised that nothing in the words of Seneca which I quoted should lead one to think that the books mentioned were books belonging to the royal library. On the contrary, it would seem clear that they were intended as a munificent gift to one of the great Roman lords of the time, whose vainglorious love of display the Stoic philosopher attacks. Why would Seneca have spoken of the Egyptian sovereigns' "taste" and "care", and why would he say that the scrolls were being collected "not for study but for display", unless he were indeed writing about gifts intended for wealthy ignoramuses? Now if you put these clues together,' he concluded, 'your question is answered: these books *chanced*, as Orosius says, to be in the port, in the *depots* next to those in which grain was stored, as Dion Cassius tells us. And this was because they were gifts from the Egyptian sovereigns to some rich Roman, as Seneca says. And he tells us that his source is Livy, who is recognised as the basis of the accounts in both Orosius and Dion Cassius.'

This is what the two friends told Amrou. As if by previous agreement, they omitted to mention that Plutarch's *Life of Caesar* includes a passage in which the biographer unaccountably claims that the fire, 'spreading from the arsenal', destroyed 'the great library'. Not that John and Philaretes wished to conceal the existence of an argument that might seem to tell against them: they were well aware that Plutarch could be confuted, that the library (if we use that name for the Museum) was not at all near the arsenals, and that Plutarch had in all probability misunderstood a reference in his source to *bibliothekas*, 'deposits of books' (Dion Cassius uses the same phrase) and had imagined a catastrophic fire in the Museum. They had already made demands enough on Amrou's patience and attention. It would be pointless, they felt, to confuse him.

As they enjoyed a moment's respite, and as Amrou inwardly and with fresh admiration ran through his companions' closely reasoned argument, Omar's envoy, just disembarked at Alexandria, came to find the emir at John's house. His entrance roused them from the silent musing into which all three had not unnaturally fallen. As their discussions had followed one another during these days of waiting, they had journeyed, so to speak, into the past, drawn by the enquiry they were pursuing. Now they were pulled abruptly back into the present. Amrou read out Omar's message:

> As for the books you mention, here is my reply. If their content is in accordance with the book of Allah, we may do without them, for in that case the book of Allah more than suffices. If, on the other hand, they contain matter not in accordance with the book of Allah, there can be no need to preserve them. Proceed, then, and destroy them.

We can easily imagine the disappointment and distress this must have caused the two men – perhaps we should say the three men. And yet, Amrou reflected, what else was to be expected from a pious bigot like Omar, a man capable, so it seemed, of preventing the Prophet from dictating a new book on his deathbed, so ardent was his belief that everything was already contained in the Koran?

John, meanwhile, was thinking of the different results that could arise from a parallel intensity of faith. In his account of the scholarly symposium, Aristeas had described how the seventy-two learned Jews answered even the most far-fetched queries of the king in terms of their belief that all took place in accordance with God's will. Now, the

Caliph's rigid reply reduced everything to the question of whether or not it accorded with God's book (Allah being his name for God). And yet the scholars had played their part in enlarging an already vast library, while the Caliph – John recollected despairingly – was a barbarian ready to sanction the destruction of that same treasure on the strength of a crude syllogism.

Since he felt that he neither should nor could remain there, Amrou left John's house in silence, avoiding empty farewells. He knew he would never set foot in it again. Obedient to the Caliph's orders, he set about his task of destruction. The books were distributed to the public baths of Alexandria, where they were used to feed the stoves which kept the baths so comfortably warm. Ibn al-Kifti writes that 'the number of baths was well known, but I have forgotten it' (we have Eutychius's word that there were in fact four thousand). 'They say', continues Ibn al-Kifti, 'that it took six months to burn all that mass of material.'

Aristotle's books were the only ones spared.

References

I

The Pharaoh's Tomb: *Iliad*, IX, 383-384 (Thebes); Diodorus Siculus, I, 46–48, 5 (Hecataeus's exploration of the Ramesseum at Thebes, as far as the Odeon).

II

The Sacred Library: Diodorus, I, 48, 6–49 (description of the second part of the Ramesseum); Plutarch, *Life of Lycurgus*, 20, 3 (Hecataeus goes to Sparta); Flavius Josephus, *Against Apion*, I, 183 (relationship between Hecataeus and Ptolemy); Photius, *Bibliotheca*, 244, p. 380, a7 (Hecataeus's excursus on the Jews).

III

The Forbidden City: Herodas, *Mimiambi*, I, 26–32 (the go-between on Cos); Theocritus, *Idylls*, XV, 133–135 (feast of Adonis); Diodorus, XVII, 52 and Strabo, XVII, 1, 8 (topography of Alexandria); Lucan, *Bellum Civile*, X, 486–488 (plan of the palace as approached from the sea); Herodotus, III, 83 (access to the sovereign's palace the privilege of a hereditary caste); Aristeas' *Letter*, 38 (the 'king's books').

IV

The Fugitive: Plutarch, *How a flatterer may be distinguished from a friend*, 69c (Demetrius Phalereus at Thebes); Plutarch, *On exile*, 601f (Ptolemy Soter's regard for Demetrius); Diogenes Laertius, V, 58 (Strato the

tutor of Ptolemy Philadelphus); Theocritus, *Idylls,* XVII, 26 (Ptolemy Soter and Alexander relatives by common descent); Strabo, XIII, 1, 54 (Aristotle 'taught the kings of Egypt how to organise a library'); Plutarch, *Short sayings of kings and commanders,* 189d (Demetrius urges Ptolemy to read 'books on kingship'); Aelian, *Historia varia,* III, 17 (Demetrius suggests legislation to Ptolemy); Theocritus, *Idylls,* XVII, 34-44 (Berenice favoured by Ptolemy Soter); Diogenes Laertius, V, 78 (Demetrius intervenes to oppose Ptolemy's plan to share his throne with Philadelphus); Hermippus (*ibid.*) (arrest and death of Demetrius); Cicero, *Pro Rabirio Postumo,* 23 (murder of Demetrius Phalereus).

V

The Universal Library: Aristeas' *Letter,* 9–10 (Ptolemy's visit to the library); Tzetzes, *De comoedia,* Koster p. 43 (collection and translation of books from 'all the peoples of the world'); Epiphanius, *De mensuris et ponderibus* (in Migne, *Patrologia Graeca,* XLIII, p. 252) (Ptolemy's letter to 'all the sovereigns on earth'); Galen, XVII. 1, Kühn p. 601 (the 'ships' collection'); Aristeas' *Letter,* 29-30 (Demetrius's written reports to Ptolemy on the growth of the library) and 11 (the decision to acquire and translate the Old Testament); Flavius Josephus, *Against Apion,* II, 35 (Jewish quarter of Alexandria near the palace), II, 36 and 42 (allocation of this district to the Jews by Alexander) and 176 (form in which parchment texts were kept); II *Maccabees* 4, 13 ('Hellenisation'); Aristeas' *Letter,* 12 (Aristeas' relations with Sosibius of Tarentum and Andrew) and 6 (his earlier writings on the Jews); Pliny, *Naturalis historia,* XXX, 4 (translation and indexing of texts attributed to Zoroaster); Seneca, *Suasoriae,* I, 10 (Alexander at 'the limits of the world'); Chronicle of Maribas the Armenian (in *Journal Asiatique,* May–June 1903, pp. 492-493) (Alexander's plans for a library at Nineveh).

VI

'I leave my books to Neleus': Diogenes Laertius, V, 52 (Theophrastus's will) and V, 39 (Demetrius's aid to the peripatetic school); Strabo,

XIII, 1, 54 (Neleus's background and his removal to Scepsis); the *Vita Marciana* of Aristotle, Düring p. 97 (Proxenus of Atarneus tutors Aristotle); Demosthenes, X, 32 and Didymus, *Commentary on Demosthenes*, col. 5 (fate of Hermias); Diogenes Laertius, V, 58 (Strato elected scholarch); Athenaeus, I, 3A (record at Alexandria of the acquisition of the books of Aristotle and Theophrastus).

VII

The Symposium: Aristeas' *Letter*, 15–23 (freeing of the Jews deported to Egypt), 37 (Ptolemy Philadelphus's letter to Eleazar), 41–42 (Eleazar's reply), 107–111 (Jerusalem and Alexandria), 187–294 (the symposium and the seventy-two translators); Diogenes Laertius, II, 129–130 and 140 and Tertullian, *Apologetics* 18 (Menedemus in Egypt); *Papyrus Oxyrhyncus* 2382 (fragment of a Hellenistic tragedy based on the episode of Gyges and Candaules); Eusebius, *Praeparatio Evangelica*, IX, 27–28 (Ezekiel's Jewish tragedy); Aristeas' *Letter*, 316 (Theodectes' unsuccessful attempt to compose a tragedy on a Jewish theme) and 301–302 (Demetrius oversees the transcription of the translated passages of the Old Testament).

VIII

In the Cage of the Muses: Timon of Phlius, frag. 12, Diels (corresp. Athenaeus, I, 22 D) ('the cage of the Muses'); *Orientis Graeci inscriptiones Selectae*, 714, *Berliner Griechische Urkunden* III, 729, 1, Philostratus, *Lives of the Sophists*, 1, 22, 3 and 22, 5 and Dion Cassius, LXXVII, 7 (material privileges of the members of the Museum); Diogenes Laertius, IX, 113 (Timon's dislike of Zenodotus's Homeric criticism); *Iliad* IV, 88, scholium A (arguments against the authenticity of this line, attributed to Zenodotus); *Iliad* I, 4–5, scholium A, Aristonicus (Zenodotus's suggestion that these two lines should be omitted); Vitruvius, VII, pref., 5–7 (plagiarists exposed by Aristophanes of Byzantium, who has a deep knowledge of the library); Suidas, under 'Callimachus' (titles and extent of Callimachus's catalogues); the 'French scholar' referred to is Edmond Saglio: see the article 'Bibliotheca' in the *Dictionnaire des*

Antiquités grecques et romaines (p. 707); John Philoponus, *Commentary on Aristotle's Categories* (corresp. *Commentaria in Aristotelem Graeca*, XIII, 1), p. 7 and Olympiodorus, *Prolegomena* (corresp. *ibid*, XII, 1), p. 13 (forged and erroneously attributed Aristotelian texts flood into Alexandria); Diogenes Laertius, V, 80–81 (Demetrius Phalereus's treatises on the *Iliad*, the *Odyssey* and Homer); Proclus, *Commentary on the Timaeus*, 21 c (Plato sends for the text of Antimachus); Aristotle, *Poetics*, 1459b 1–6 (Homer's *Iliad* and *Odyssey* counterposed to the poems of the epic cycle); *Iliad*, XII, 435, scholium A (Aristarchus's polemic *Against Xenon's Paradox*, in other words against the view that the *Iliad* and the *Odyssey* were written by two different authors); Callimachus, *Epigrams*, 28, 1-2 (against 'cyclical poems') and Proem to *Aitia* (against the 'Telchines'); Dionysus of Halicarnassus, *On Demosthenes*, 13 and *On Dinarchus*, 10, and Photius, *Bibliotheca*, 265, p. 491b 31 (severe strictures regarding Callimachus's catalogues in the domain of Attic oratory); Callimachus, *Epigrams*, 55, 4 (lines modelled on *Isaiah*, 14, 12); Vitruvius, VII, pref., 8–9 (sentence passed on Zoilus); Suidas, under 'Callimachus' (his poem, *Ibis*, against Apollonius) and under 'Aristophanes the Grammarian' (Aristophanes of Byzantium attempts to flee from Alexandria).

IX

The Rival Library: Galen, *Commentary on Hippocrates*, XV, Kühn pp. 105–107 (production of forgeries stimulated by the rivalry between Pergamum and Alexandria); final additional text below the speech *On Halonnesus* in Paris Greek codex 2934 (folio 29r) (where it is stated that the edition of Demosthenes originating in Pergamum comprised six speeches in each scroll); note added to col. 15 in papyrus Berlin inv. 9780 (Didymus's *Commentary*) (where it is stated that the Alexandrian edition of Demosthenes comprised three or at most four speeches to each scroll); *ibid.*, col. 11, 10ff. (the revelation that the eleventh Philippic attributed to Demosthenes was in fact found in the seventh book of the *Philippika* of Anaximenes of Lampsacus); Didymus, apud Marcellinus, *Life of Thucydides*, 31–34 (on Zopyrus and Cratippus); Galen, *Commentary on the third book of the 'Epidemics'*, II, 4 (the claim that Ptolemy Euergetes played a trick on the Athenians); John of Lydia, *De mensibus,* I, 28 (ban on the export of papyrus aimed against Pergamum); Hermogenes, in Spengel, *Rhetores Graeci,* II, pp. 352. 28–354. 3 (passages struck out of Demosthenes' *Crown*); *Iliad,* XVIII, 483, scholium by Aristonicus (Zenodotus's condemnation of the entire description of Achilles' arms as inauthentic); *Iliad,* XI, 40, scholium T (allegorical interpretation of Achilles' shield, advanced by Crates of Mallus).

X

Reappearance and Disappearance of Aristotle: Posidonius, Jacoby fragment 36 (Athenion's career and his relationship with Apellicon); Plutarch, *Life of Sulla,* 26 (Tyrannion and Andronicus grappling with the Aristotelian texts); Strabo, XIII, 1, 54 (Tyrannion gains temporary possession of Apellicon's scrolls); Seneca, *De tranquillitate animi,* 9, 5 (bibliophilia among the rich at Rome); Cicero, *Ad Atticum,* IV, 10 (April, 55 BC) (letter to Atticus from Faustus's library).

XI

The Second Visitor: Diodorus Siculus, I, 83, 8–9 (summary execution of the Roman who killed the cat); Strabo, XVII, 1, 8 (profanation of Alexander's tomb by Ptolemy 'the clandestine'); Suetonius, *Life of Caesar,* 54, 3 (Caesar given six thousand talents by Ptolemy); Polybius, XII, 27 (historians who work from books in libraries); Diodorus, I, 4, 1 (his fabricated voyages) and XVII, 52 (the riches of Alexandria); Pliny, *Naturalis Historia,* Pref., 25 (praise of Diodorus for the frankness of his chosen title); Aphthonius, *Progymnasmata,* 12 (Walz p. 107); Diodorus, I, 46, 7 (plan of the Ramesseum taken from Hecataeus).

XII

War: Plutarch, *Life of Caesar,* 49 (Caesar's visit to Alexandria, and the outbreak of conflict following the unsuccessful plot in the palace); Lucan, *Bellum civile,* X, 439–454 (Caesar hemmed in in the royal palace at Alexandria); Dion Cassius, XLII, 38, 1 (Roman deserters in Ptolemy's army); Lucan, X, 486–505 (Caesar, from the palace above, sets fire to the ships); Dion Cassius, XLII, 38, 2 (the fire takes hold of the 'depots of grain and books'); Orosius, VI, 15, 31 (the books that were burned lay in the port area 'by chance'); Caesar, *Bellum civile*, III, 111 (the burning of the ships); *Bellum Alexandrinum*, 1 (highly fire-resistant properties of the building materials used at Alexandria).

XIII
The Third Visitor: Plutarch, *Life of Antony*, 58 and 59 (Calvisius insinuates that Antony planned to take books from Pergamum to Alexandria); Suetonius, *Life of Caesar*, 35, 1 (Caesar's reluctance to make Egypt a province of the Empire); Dessau, *Inscriptiones Latinae Selectae* 8995 (the Elephantina inscription); Strabo, XVII, 1, 46 (Strabo comes to Egypt with Aelius Gallus), XVII, 1, 45 (the Indian snake presented to Augustus) and XVII, 1, 5 (his discussion of the flow of the Nile and the texts he consulted on the question); Diodorus, I, 38–41 (Agatharchides' theories on the matter); Seneca, *Epistulae ad Lucilium*, 88, 37 (Didymus's works amount to four thousand scrolls); Pliny, *Naturalis Historia*, Pref., 25 (Tiberius's admiration of Apion the grammarian); Strabo, I, 2, 31 (Aristonicus of Alexandria); Photius, *Bibliotheca*, 161, p. 104b 40–41 (Aristonicus's treatise on the Alexandrian Museum); Strabo, XVII, 1, 8 (description of the Alexandrian Museum).

XIV
The Library: Diodorus, I, 47–49.

XV
The Fire: Aphthonius, *Progymnasmata*, 12 (Walz p. 107) (plan of the Serapeum).

XVI
The Dialogue of John Philoponus with the Emir: Amrou's letter to the Caliph is cited in Eutychius's *Annals* (II, Pococke's ed. p. 316). The basis of the dialogue between John and Amrou will be found in

Ibn al-Kifti's book *Ta'rikh al-Hukama* ('Chronicle of wise men'). The texts invoked during the discussion of the fire supposed to have taken place during the Alexandrian war of Caesar are those cited above, in the note on Chapter XII, and also the following: Seneca, *De Tranquillitate animi*, 9, 5; Ammianus, XXII, 16, 13; Gellius, VII, 17, 3; and (on Caracalla's threat to destroy the Museum and its inhabitants) Dion Cassius, LXXVII, 7.

PART II

THE SOURCES

Gibbon

EDWARD Gibbon commented that if Omar really ordered the books to be burned, 'the fact is indeed marvellous' (*The Decline and Fall of the Roman Empire*, 1838 ed., vol. VI, p. 452). Gibbon's source was the *Specimen Historiae Arabum* of Gregory Abulpharagius, a thirteenth-century Jewish doctor known as Bar Hebraeus, in the seventeenth-century Latin translation (1649) made by Edward Pococke, the great orientalist of Corpus Christi College. Gibbon goes on to remark that

> the solitary report of a stranger who wrote at the end of six hundred years on the confines of Media is overbalanced by the silence of two annalists of a more early date, both Christians, both natives of Egypt, and the most ancient of whom, the patriarch Eutychius [AD 876–940], has amply described the conquest of Alexandria.

He notes also the 'silence of Abulfeda, Murtadi, and a crowd of Moslems'. He then comments:

> The rigid sentence of Omar is repugnant to the sound and orthodox precept of the Mahometan casuists: they expressly

declare, that the religious books of the Jews and Christians, which are acquired by the right of war, should never be committed to the flames.

His authority here is Hadrianus Reland, the distinguished Dutch Arabist who lived at the end of the seventeenth century. In his *De jure militari Mohammedanorum*, Reland explains that the religious books of Jews and Christians were not burned for reasons 'derived from the respect that is due to the *name* of God'.

Gibbon does not question the view that John Philoponus was still alive when the Arabs conquered Alexandria, a view founded on the Arabic sources, beginning with the important *Index* (*al-Fihrist*) made by the son of 'al-Warraq' ('the bookseller'), which lists every Arabic book and translation into Arabic that its compiler had examined up until the year 988. This dating accords with what we can infer from Philoponus's commentary on the fourth book of Aristotle's *Physics*, where he remarks: 'I set it down that today is the tenth of May of the year 333 since the beginning of the reign of Diocletian' (*Commentaria in Aristotelem Graeca*, vol. XVII, Berlin 1888, p. 703). Unfortunately, however, some ambiguity attaches to this piece of evidence. The year is given as 333 in several codices, including some of the best, such as the twelfth-century Laurentian MS 87. 6. But it appears as 233 in the fourteenth- or fifteenth-century Greek Marcian MS 230 — written, according to Vitelli, who prepared the Berlin edition, 'rather carelessly'. The first figure corresponds to 617, and the second to 517, in the Christian calendar. Fabricius, the authority whom

Gibbon follows, took the remark in the commentary on the *Physics* as confirming the Arabic sources, which state that Philoponus was alive in 640 AD and that he conversed with Amrou. Elsewhere in his works, however – to be precise, in the sixteenth book of his polemic *Against Proclus on the Eternity of the World* – Philoponus writes: 'And now in our times, in the year 245 since Diocletian's reign.' Fabricius, appealing to the general sense of the passage in which this phrase occurs, suggested that the time indication was to be understood 'rather loosely' (*paulo laxius*), and that Philoponus's words should be rendered 'Nam et non longe a nostris temporibus anno 245 Diocletiani' ('Now not long from our own times, in the year 245 of Diocletian') (*Bibliotheca Graeca*, vol. X, p. 644 in Harles' revised edition). The fact remains that the presence in Simplicius's commentary on Aristotle's *De caelo* of certain quotations from the *Replies to Aristotle on the Eternity of the World* (a lost work attributed to Philoponus) inclined scholars as early as the eighteenth century to prefer the less recent date and to regard the supposed meeting between Philoponus and Amrou as the consequence of confusion in the Arabic sources.

John Philoponus's work was well known to the Arabs, and played an important part in the spread of Aristotle's thought during the early centuries of Arabic culture. This must be the basis of the connection between Philoponus and Amrou which figures in the Arabic historical sources. Ibn al-Kifti relates the dialogue in which John gives a summary account of the opening episode of Aristeas' *Letter*, the meeting between Ptolemy and Demetrius in the library precincts (an English version of this passage, from the Arabic text prepared by Hussein Mones, is given by Edward A. Parsons, *The Alexandrian Library*, New York 1952, pp. 389–392). The name Philaretes is found in certain manuscripts containing the Latin translation of Philoponus's work on *Pulsations* (Fabricius, *Bibliotheca Graeca*, X, p. 652).

Gibbon's aim, as a man of the enlightenment, was to acquit the Arabs of a crime they had never in his view committed. He sought to lay the blame for the destruction of the library on the shoulders of Caesar, who had wrought such havoc during the Alexandrian war, and above all on the terrible archbishop Theophilus, who razed the Serapeum and whom Gibbon describes as 'the perpetual enemy of peace and virtue; a bold, bad man, whose hands were alternately polluted with gold, and with blood' (*Decline and Fall*, III, 519): Gibbon here confuses the palace library with the library in the Serapeum, an error in which he follows Tertullian (*Apologetics*, 18, 8) and above all Ammianus Marcellinus (XXII, 16). 'I shall not recapitulate', he writes,

> the disasters of the Alexandrian library, the involuntary flame that was kindled by Caesar in his own defence, or the mischievous bigotry of the Christians who studied to destroy the monuments of idolatry. . . . But if the ponderous mass of Arian and Monophysite controversy were indeed consumed in the public baths, a philosopher may allow, with a smile, that it was ultimately devoted to the benefit of mankind (VI, 452 f.).

For Gibbon, the fate of the great libraries of antiquity is linked above all to the history of the classical textual tradition. In the spirit of Voltaire, he draws a positive

balance even at the foot of this melancholy record of fanatical despoliation and human folly. He betrays a certain teleological optimism, and sets a low value on what has been lost:

> I sincerely regret the more valuable libraries which have been involved in the ruin of the Roman empire; but when I seriously compute the lapse of ages, the waste of ignorance, and the calamities of war, our treasures, rather than our losses, are the object of my surprise.

And he then goes on to write in terms which make clear his sense of tradition, his evaluation of what has perished, and the characteristics or criteria which have in his view determined the survival of certain works:

> Many curious and interesting facts are buried in oblivion; the three great historians of Rome have been transmitted to our hands in a mutilated state, and we are deprived of many pleasing compositions of the lyric, iambic and dramatic poetry of the Greeks. Yet we should gratefully remember, that the mischances of time and accident have spared the classic works to which the suffrage of antiquity [here there is a reference, in a footnote, to Quintilian's critical enumeration of classical texts] had adjudged the first place of genius and glory.

Gibbon notes, too, that the 'teachers of ancient knowledge', whose works survive, have an especial value as repositories of the knowledge of earlier times: he mentions Aristotle, the elder Pliny and Galen among those who 'had perused and compared the writings of their predecessors', and concludes:

Nor can it fairly be presumed that any important truth, any useful discovery in art or nature, has been snatched away from the curiosity of modern ages (p. 454).

The Dialogues of Amrou

ORIENTAL and Arabic tradition preserves the record of dialogues between the emir Amrou ibn el-Ass and a number of important historical figures: the Byzantine emperor, who challenged the Arab claim to the possession of Syria; Benjamin, the Jacobite patriarch of Egypt, whose favour Amrou was shrewd enough to gain; John I, Jacobite patriarch of Syria; and John Philoponus. *Patrologia Orientalis* (volume I, 1903, pp. 494–498) prints texts of the accounts of his meeting with the Egyptian patriarch. His conversation with John, patriarch of Syria, referred to at the beginning of chapter XVI above, was brought to light by the discovery in the British Museum of a Syriac manuscript (Add. MS 17193) on which the copyist finished work in August 874. Abbot François Nau, co-editor of *Patrologia Orientalis*, unearthed the manuscript, confirmed its authenticity, and published the text, together with a translation and commentary, in the *Journal Asiatique* of March–April 1915 (series XI, volume V, pp. 225–279). Nau showed that the patriarch John mentioned in the title of the dialogue must be John I, who held that position from 635 until December 648, during the time when Amrou, with the support of the disaffected subject people of the empire, was conquering Syria (Antioch fell in 638).

The text found in this miscellaneous codex (Add. MS 17193) is presented as an account of the dialogue compiled by John himself a few days after his meeting with Amrou. The date, given at the outset, corresponds to 9 May 639. (The manuscript is thus rather more than two centuries later than the dialogue it records.) Nau regards it as certain that Amrou and the Syrian patriarch really did meet, and suggests that this was a clever tactical move on the part of the emir. In 639, Amrou was still engaged in the conquest of Mesopotamia, where the Jacobite communities, monophysites following the Syriac observance, had great influence. Amrou accordingly decided to win their spiritual head over to his side.

In their dialogue, Amrou was concerned not only with Christology but also with the question whether there was one single holy book. Amrou's views have been seen as paralleling the abrupt dogmatism of Omar's verdict. 'The distinguished emir', so the patriarch relates, 'asked us whether a single gospel was held to be true by all those who profess to be Christians and who go by the name of Christians in the world.' When the patriarch replied in the affirmative, Amrou objected that in that case it was impossible to understand how Christians had become divided into the different 'faiths' to which they seemed to adhere. The patriarch's response was marked by its broad tolerance: the Pentateuch, he said, was also regarded as a sacred book by men professing different religions, such as Jews, Christians, and Moslems. Amrou then approached the issue from another angle, posing various concrete empirical questions (how, for instance, should a man divide his inheritance among his heirs?) and asking whether the Christian gospel contained answers to queries of that kind. Told that the gospel was concerned only with 'heavenly doctrine and vivifying precepts', he exhorted the patriarch, in fatherly terms, 'either to show me that your laws are contained in your gospel and thus that you regulate your lives in accordance with it, or else to follow Moslem law without more ado'. The patriarch's reply was a defence of *plurality*: 'We Christians have laws too' – that is, laws apart from the gospel – 'but these are in accord with the precepts of the gospel, the canons of the apostles and the laws of the church.'

However, and contrary to Nau's opinion, Amrou's position should not be seen as prefiguring the fatal dilemma posed by Omar. According to the Syriac historian Michael, it was after this very dialogue that the emir asked the patriarch to have the Christian gospel translated into Arabic – albeit omitting the bizarre passages referring to Christ's divinity. And when John protested at this, he gave way with good grace, saying, 'Very well, write it as you wish' (*Chronique ecclésiastique*, II, pp. 431–432). In such a conciliatory climate, it need not surprise us that the 'Moslem' gospel of Barnabas contains a variant account of the crucifixion, with Judas crucified in Christ's place. This version accords with the statement in the Koran (sura IV, 156) that 'they did not crucify him, and a man resembling him was put in his place'.

A learned Jew also took part in this colloquy between Amrou and the Jacobite patriarch of Syria. He had been called in by Amrou, who wanted to establish the original Hebrew reading of a passage in _Genesis_ (19, 24) in which the word 'Lord' occurs twice ('Then the LORD rained upon Sodom and upon Gomorrah brimstone and fire from the LORD out of heaven'). The passage, evidently, furnishes rare opportunities for Christological dispute. Asked whether the text read thus in the Jewish Law, the learned Jew replied, according to the patriarch's account, that he 'could not say with certainty'.

3

Revisions of Aristeas

IN his record of the dialogue between Amrou and John Philoponus, the Egyptian-born Arab historian Ibn al-Kifti gives John a long speech in which the origin and history of the library at Alexandria are recalled. A good part of this is freely adapted from Aristeas' *Letter*, but there is one significant change. In Aristeas' *Letter*, Demetrius assures his sovereign that the planned total of 500,000 scrolls will 'soon' be reached (paragraph 10), and draws his attention only to the special case of the 'Jewish Law'. In Ibn al-Kifti's account, however, when the king, told that 54,000 books have now been collected, asks 'How many do we still lack?', he receives a much more disquieting reply. Zamira (the Arabic form of 'Demetrius') lists the peoples whose books must be acquired before the library can be called 'complete': the inhabitants of 'northern India, India, Persia, Georgia, Armenia, Babylon, Musalla, the territory of Rum [Byzantium]'.

An exactly similar reworking of Aristeas' account is found at the beginning of the *De mensuris et ponderibus* of Bishop Epiphanius (315–403 AD), who became Metropolitan of Cyprus in his old age. Epiphanius's remarkable work has been called a 'biblische Realencyklopädie' (Altaner and Stuiber, *Patrologie*, Freiburg-Basel-Wien, 1966 [seventh ed.], p. 316). It consists, first of all, of an account of the translation into Greek of the Old Testament. Within this pithy and valuable discussion, the author – as was, indeed, quite customary – indulges in a digression concerning the library at Alexandria. Having already mentioned Ptolemy Philadelphus, in whose reign the seventy-two translators carried out their task, Epiphanius continues as follows:

> The second sovereign of Alexandria after Ptolemy, to wit the king known as Ptolemy Philadelphus, was a man who loved beauty and culture. He founded a library in this same city of Alexandria, in the district known as Bruchion (a quarter now altogether abandoned), and he put one Demetrius Phalereus in charge of it, instructing him to collect together all the books of the world. . . . The work proceeded, and books were gathered from all parts, until one day the king asked the director of the library how many books had been collected. The director replied: 'There are about 54,800. We hear, however, that there is a great quantity of books among the Ethiopians, the Indians, the Persians, the Elamites, the Babylonians, the Chaldaeans, the Romans, the Phoenicians and the Syrians.' [Here Epiphanius inserts a parenthesis, remarking that 'at that time the Romans did not yet bear that name, and were called Latins'. He then gives Demetrius's words once more.] 'At Jerusalem, in Judea, too, there are sacred books that speak of God . . .' (*Patrologia Graeca*, volume 43, cols. 250 and 252).

Epiphanius then recounts the exchange of letters between Ptolemy and Eleazar. Here, too, Aristeas' text is reworked:

among other changes, the king's letter is addressed not to Eleazar in person but to the Jews in general. Ibn al-Kifti, for his part, omits all reference to the Jews.

The two lists of peoples are worth commenting on. In Epiphanius, we find a mixture of peoples known in Biblical tradition (Elamites, Assyrians-Babylonians, and so on) and 'present-day' places (Rome, Ethiopia, India). The Arab chronicler includes places (Georgia, Armenia) within the sphere of Arabic rule and influence. In these ways, the original list is brought up to date.

Ibn al-Kifti makes use of Epiphanius's work, taking from it the figure of 54,000 which he gives as the number of scrolls collected in the library at Alexandria in the reign of Ptolemy Philadelphus (the figure appears nowhere else in the extensive body of material derived from Aristeas). He modifies his source in some places, and interprets it in others. One instance is the reference to the Romans. 'The Romans', for Epiphanius, were the inhabitants of Latium or Italy, and he therefore adds a note to inform his readers that they were at one time called 'Latins'. Ibn al-Kifti can have made little of this note, for to him *Romaioi* meant 'Byzantines', that being the usage current in his world. The Byzantines were Greeks. Ironically, then, successive reworkings of Aristeas culminated in this version given by the medieval Arab chronicler according to which the library at Alexandria actually lacked the books of the Greeks.

Only part of Epiphanius's book is preserved in Greek, but the whole work survives in Syriac translation (Altaner and Stuiber, p. 316). It was highly regarded in Arabic culture, and enjoyed a wide currency. Among those who made good use of it was the author of the Preface to the Arabic version of the Pentateuch (the text of which was published in Latin translation in 1692 in Oxford, in the volume entitled *Aristeae Historia LXX interpretum*, p. 131).

4

Aulus Gellius

GIBBON, like many subsequent scholars, draws his data about the destruction of the library of Alexandria from Ammianus Marcellinus (XXII, 16, 13), the Antiochene historian and admirer of Julian the Apostate. However, quite apart from the fact that Ammianus confuses the royal library with the library in the Serapeum (a point already mentioned: he tries to escape his own confusion by saying that there are *several* valuable libraries — *bybliothecae inaestimabiles,* — in the Serapeum), he cannot be regarded as an independent source. His account is derived from the *Attic Nights* of Aulus Gellius (VII, 17), where we read that

> Pisistratus, the Tyrant, is said to have been the first to make books concerning the liberal arts available to the public to read. Afterwards, the Athenians themselves built up the collection with care and toil. But when Xerxes occupied Athens and burned the city apart from the Acropolis, he stole all this wealth of books and took them away with him to Persia. Much later King Seleucus, known as Nicanor, had all these books restored to Athens.
>
> Afterwards a very great many books were collected or made in Egypt, by the Ptolemies; as many as seven hundred

thousand scrolls. But in the course of the first war of Alexandria, during the sack of the city, all these thousands of scrolls were given to the flames: not spontaneously, to be sure, nor by intention, but accidentally, by the auxiliaries.

Ammianus, for his part, writes that 'the seven hundred thousand scrolls so laboriously and indefatigably collected by the Ptolemies were burned in the war of Alexandria, during the sack of the city, under the dictatorship of Caesar'. He uses the same words as Gellius, except that he alters, or rather glosses, the phrase *bello priore Alexandrino dum diripitur ea civitas* to read *bello Alexandrino, dum diripitur civitas sub dictatore Caesare*.

From the summary given at its beginning, however, it seems that Gellius's chapter originally included no reference to the library at Alexandria. (These summaries, written by the author, appear at the end of the general preface, giving an overall picture of the work's contents; and each then reappears in its place at the head of the successive chapters.) The summary promises an account of 'who first founded a public library and how many books there were in Athens in the public libraries before the defeats in the Persian wars'. There is nothing about the second part of the chapter, which deals with Alexandria. And this second part is clumsily tacked onto the first, giving the impression that Ptolemy came after Seleucus in terms of chronology.

The author of this second part had, moreover, a remarkably precise idea of those responsible for the burning of the library: they were, he informs us unequivocally, certain *milites auxiliarii*, 'auxiliaries'. As we know (from the *Bellum Alexandrinum*), Caesar was helped, during the Alexandrian

conflict, by the arrival of troops under prince Mithridates of Pergamum who came to his support. The author of the interpolated passage obviously took the view that the terrible destruction of books could not have been perpetrated by Romans.

We need hardly point out that he, too, refers to the mythical 'sack of Alexandria'. He is further discredited by his complete failure to take account of the precise details about the circumstances and spread of the fire which were readily available both in the *Bellum Alexandrinum* and in the many sources based on Livy (see chapter III above).

5

Isidore of Seville

O F the two parts of Gellius's chapter, the first dealing with Athens and the second with Alexandria,
Ammianus uses (and slightly modifies) only the second.

Isidore of Seville, by contrast, uses only the first. In his
encyclopaedic work on *Etymologies,* in the chapter entitled,
precisely, *De bibliothecis,* he writes (VI, 3, 3) as follows:

> *On libraries.* Library, *bibliotheca,* is a word of Greek origin:
> the term derives from the fact that books are kept there. We
> can translate: *biblion,* of books; *theke,* depository. 2. After the
> books of the Law were burned by the Chaldaeans, the library
> of the Old Testament was restored by Esdras, inspired by the
> Holy Spirits; he corrected every volume of the Law and the
> Prophets, which had been corrupted by the Gentiles, and
> established the entire Old Testament in twenty-two books,
> in such a way that the number of books might correspond
> with the number of letters. 3. Among the Greeks, on the
> other hand, it is thought that Pisistratus, tyrant of Athens,
> was the first to found a library: this library, subsequently built
> up by the Athenians, was taken to Persia by Xerxes, after the
> burning of Athens: much later, Seleucus Nicanor returned it
> to Greece. 4. And from here grew the fashion, known among

all sovereigns and in every city, for obtaining the books of various peoples and, by the work of translators, turning them into Greek. 5. This is why Alexander the Great, or perhaps his successors, set about building libraries in which every book would be contained. And Ptolemy called Philadelphus, in particular, who was deeply versed in letters and who vied with Pisistratus in his devotion to libraries, brought together in his library not only the works of the gentiles but the holy scriptures too. In fact, seventy thousand volumes were to be found in Alexandria in those days.

There follows a chapter entitled *De interpretibus,* which opens with the story, derived from Aristeas, of the seventy-two translators of the Old Testament.

Isidore thus draws on Gellius in his discussion of Pisistratus. In the sequel he no longer does so, even though he, like Gellius, goes on to discuss Alexandria and its scrolls. This may be mere chance. However, it is not unlikely that Isidore's edition of Gellius, early in the seventh century, did not yet include the section on Alexandria in chapter 17 of Book VII.

In that case, how can Ammianus, three centuries before Isidore, possibly have known it? Ammianus may in fact have had access not to Gellius, but simply to the source also used by the author of the interpolated passage in Gellius.

Now even though the two passages under consideration – the one in Gellius, the other in Isidore – very clearly share a common element (the history of Pisistratus's library), the prevailing view of modern scholars is that they derive from two different sources (both of which are lost), namely

Varro's *De bibliothecis* in the former case and Suetonius's *De viris illustribus* in the second. This scholarly consensus is all the more surprising given that neither author makes any reference to the sources he is using.

Why are such venerable antecedents ascribed to the two passages? The reason is not far to seek: such antecedents enhance their standing as historical evidence. So eminent an authority as Carl Wendel, for instance, has described Gellius's account of the library at Alexandria as laying 'sole claim to historical validity', and he argues that we can thus be confident that 'at the moment when the library was burned its scrolls numbered seven hundred thousand' (see Milkau-Leyh, *Handbuch der Bibliothekswissenschaft*, III, 1 [second ed.], Wiesbaden 1955, p. 69). However, Peter Marshall Fraser, an authoritative but lonely voice, has commented more recently that the figure given by Gellius and Ammianus certainly deserves less credence than other figures (*Ptolemaic Alexandria*, Oxford 1972, II, p. 493, note 224).

Wendel, in a simplified version of the general view which he does not support by any detailed discussion, derives the passage in both Gellius and Isidore from Varro's treatise. Why choose Varro? Caesar, as is well known, formally appointed Varro to the 'care of the library' (*cura bibliothecarum*: Suetonius, *Life of Caesar*, 44). A careful scholar and a great collector of books, Varro prepared for his task by making a series of studies of the topic. The fruit of his labours was the *De bibliothecis*. This is the basis on which modern scholarship has built, arriving at its present view by the following not entirely logical series of steps. Pliny (*Naturalis Historia*,

XIII, 68–70), discussing the writing materials used in the Greco-Roman world, cites an absurd theory, attributed (perhaps wrongly) to Varro, that papyrus-leaf was adopted only at the time of 'the victory of Alexander the Great', a theory which Pliny soon proceeds to demolish. Because Isidore likewise devotes certain chapters of his sixth Book (9–12) to the topic of writing materials (*de ceris, de cartis, de pergamenis, de libris conficiendis:* 'on writing-tablets, paper, parchment and the making of books'), the inference has been drawn that he must depend on Varro by way of Suetonius (he cites Suetonius elsewhere, in an entirely different connection). Dahlmann, for example, advances this thesis in his article on *Marcus Terentius Varro* in the 'Pauly-Wissowa' Encyclopedia (VIth Supplement (1935), column 1221). Reifferschied, the editor of Suetonius's *Reliquiae* (1860), went so far as to include these chapters among Suetonius's 'remains'.

The fact is that on an essential point Isidore says exactly the contrary of Varro: *cartarum usum primum Aegyptus ministravit*, 'the Egyptians were the first to make use of paper' (VI, 10, 1).

Their extreme eagerness to recover at least some part of Varro's text has led scholars to conclude that every piece of information about books and libraries found in later writers must derive from him – including (Dahlmann argued) the chapter of Isidore entitled *de bibliothecis* (VI, 3). The paradoxical conclusion has even been reached that the chapter should be attributed not to Isidore but to 'Suetonius *apud* Isidore' (see Marshall's Oxford edition of Gellius, Volume 1, Oxford 1968, p. 272).

The passage of Isidore actually has points of contact with texts of quite another kind, above all Tertullian's *Apologetics* (18, 5), where we read:

Ptolemy called Philadelphus, who was deeply versed in letters and who vied (as I believe) with Pisistratus in his devotion to libraries [thus far the text is the same as Isidore, VI, 3, 5], among other documents whose age or curious interest made them worthy of preservation, asked also – on the suggestion of Demetrius Phalereus, a grammarian much esteemed at that time, whom he appointed to an official position – for books from the Jews ... [there follows a paraphrase of the celebrated passage in Aristeas' *Letter*].

The same text is reflected in Jerome's letters (Letter XXXIV, to Marcella): Jerome writes that the blessed Pamphilus, who wanted to build a sacred library, *cum Demetrium Phalereum et Pisistratum in sacrae bibliothecae studio vellet aequare* ('wanted to rival Demetrius Phalereus and Pisistratus in the care he devoted to his sacred library').

Here again, then, the references to ancient libraries revolve around the central episode of the translation of the Old Testament as recounted by Aristeas – with whose narrative Tertullian was quite familiar. We find exactly the same thing in Isidore (VI, 3 and 4: *de bibliothecis, de interpretibus*): Isidore, like Tertullian, inserts Gellius's remark about Pisistratus (but not what he says about the destruction of the Museum, for this passage was unknown to him) into a context whose main event is the translation of the Old Testament as recounted by Aristeas. He here reflects a tradition which seems to have little in common with either Varro or Suetonius.

At least three textual parallels can be found to passages in Isidore's *de bibliothecis* (VI, 3): Gellius, VII, 17, 1–2 (paralleled in VI, 3, 3); Tzetzes, *De comoedia*, p. 43 in Koster's edition, 11–13 (paralleled in VI, 4, where we are told that the books not just of the Jews but of all other peoples were translated); and Tertullian, *Apologetics*, 18, 5 (paralleled in VI, 5, in the account of the translation of the Old Testament). It is probable that these three sources were found alongside one another in the text actually consulted by Isidore.

6
Livy

I N his *De tranquillitate animi* (9, 5), Seneca ascribes to
Livy a comment on the loss of 40,000 scrolls in the
fire started by Caesar at Alexandria. This includes the
phrase *regiae opulentiae monumentum,* 'testimony to the
wealth of the royal house'. The same phrase, slightly
modified, recurs in Orosius's account (VI, 15, 31)
of the same episode. We can thus identify Livy as
the source of Orosius's narrative (see Chapter XVI
above).

Both texts also give the figure of 'forty thousand'. It has
been mistakenly suggested that this figure should be cor-
rected in the passage from Seneca. The suggestion, put
forward by Pincianus, has met with undue favour: Carl
Wendel (*Handbuch der Bibliothekswissenschaft,* III, 1 [sec-
ond ed.], p. 69. note 5) is among those who have given it
their unconditional support. The correction is based on the
conflicting figure that can be found in Orosius. However,
many texts of the *Historiae adversus Paganos* do read *XL milia
librorum,* 'forty thousand books': these include the excellent
codex Laurentianus 65. 1, placed by Carl Zangermeister at
the head of his list of the best codices of Orosius.

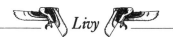

There is another set of parallels, where we find variant forms of the same expression:

Orosius: *Ea flamma cum partem quoque urbis invasisset quadraginta milia librorum* proximis *forte* aedibus *condita exussit* ('when the flames also invaded part of the city they consumed forty thousand books that chanced to be in the *buildings close by*').

Florus (*Epitoma de Tito Livio*, II, 13, 59): *ac primum* proximorum aedificiorum *atque navalium incendio infestorum hostium tela submovit* ('and the fire in the *nearby buildings* and the arsenal first drew off the weapons of the enemy').

Lucan (*Bellum Civile*, X, 498–505): *Sed quae* vicina *fuere* tecta *mari, longis rapuere vaporibus ignem. . . . Illa lues paulum clausa revocavit ab aula, urbis in auxilium, populos* ('But the fire seized hold of those *buildings* that were *close* to the sea, wrapping them in tongues of smoke. . . . This disaster soon drew the people back from the courtyard to the defence of the city').

Proximae aedes, proxima aedificia, vicina tecta are all clearly derived from whatever expression was used by Livy, the source of all three accounts. Moreover, Florus (*infestorum hostium tela submovit*) and Lucan (*clausa revocavit ab aula populos*) use similar expressions to convey how the fire's spread drew the besieging force away from the palace.

Dion Cassius (XLII, 38, 2) allows us to form a clearer picture of these 'buildings close to the sea'. The fire, he tells us, seized hold, 'among other things', of 'the arsenal (*to neorion*) and the depots where grain and books were stored'. His phraseology parallels Florus's (*proximorum aedificiorum atque navalium incendio*), so that if *navalia* corresponds to

Dion's *to neorion*, 'arsenal', then the *proxima aedificia* are the 'depots where grain and books were stored'. As well as giving us a better idea of the nature of the *proxima aedificia*, this further parallel confirms that Dion, too, was following Livy in this part of his account of the civil war.

There is no doubt that the expression used by Dion Cassius (*to neorion tas te apothekas kai tou sitou kai ton biblon*) refers to 'depots', for grain and books are conjointly mentioned, and were clearly stored quite close together. Elsewhere, admittedly, Dion Cassius (XLIX, 43, 8 and LIII, 1, 3) uses the term *apothekai biblion* to denote the *libraries* founded by Augustus, but this should not tempt us into erroneous inferences (see Dziatzko's article, *Bibliotheken*, in the Pauly-Wissowa encyclopedia, column 411, 60): *bibliotheke*, as we know, refers not to a building but to shelves. (This is of course why the plural form is often used: it is hard to see why Wendel, p. 75, note 6, should attribute Dion's usage, *apothekai biblion*, to rhetorical affectation.) In a dissertation written in Berlin in 1837 and awarded a prize by the Academy of Sciences, Gustav Parthey clearly and convincingly showed that Dion was referring to 'depots' (see *Das Alexandrinische Museum*, pp. 32–33). Parthey, an excellent Arabist, had made a long study of Alexandria's topography. He realised that the library could not have been damaged in Caesar's fire. The Museum, he concluded, had remained intact throughout the Alexandrian war but the books, removed for obscure reasons to warehouses near the port, had been devoured by the flames. He rightly stressed that Orosius (VI, 15:

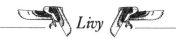

proximis forte *aedibus*) had said that the books were there 'by chance', and suggested – without claiming to resolve the issue – that Caesar had perhaps cleared the Museum of its contents and had the scrolls taken to the harbour so that they could be shipped to Rome. This hypothesis was advanced with considerable diffidence (Parthey in fact remarked that the books might have been in the depots 'for whatever reason someone else cares to think up'), and it is in truth very fragile. The sequence of events between Caesar's arrival in Alexandria and his firing of the ships moored in the port, as this is recorded in the final chapters of the third commentary *De bello civili*, hardly left him the leisure, trapped as he was in a situation of grave danger, to dream up Napoleonic schemes (Parthey may have been influenced by the example of Napoleon's cultural plundering of Egypt). There is no need to think that the books burned in the depots near the port were from the Museum: we know from our earlier discussion (Chapter XVI above) that the context in Seneca (*De tranquillitate animi*, 9, 5) clearly points to books of quite another sort. An amusing instance of the innumerable confusions that bedevil modern scholarly interpretations of the episode is found in Dziatzko (column 413, 1–5), who transforms Parthey's tentative suggestion into a certainty: Dziatzko writes, 'In the year 47 BC most of the book collection was burned. Caesar had intended to transport these books to Rome (Parthey, p. 32).'

The surviving tradition which derives from Livy (this includes Dion) permits us to obtain a clear idea of Livy's relation of the story. The parallel between Orosius, Florus and Lucan identifies the phrase *proximae aedes* as Livy's; the parallel between Florus and Dion allows us to trace a further detail – that these *aedes* were the arsenals and port depots – to Livy too.

The identification of a part of these *aedes* as book depots is consistent with Orosius's comment that the burned books were there *forte*, 'by chance': they were stored in depots, in other words, like any other kind of goods. Livy must also be credited, then, with this vital additional detail.

Putting together these pieces of the mosaic, we are led to conclude that Livy, when he spoke of books burned in the conflagration, never suggested that they were treasures from the library consumed in the (non-existent) fire in the Museum. He spoke of them, rather, as scrolls intended for the commercial market, destroyed by chance in the flames that engulfed the port and its environs. It is no oversight, then, that the epitome or *Periocha* to book CXII, packed as it is with Egyptian incidents, makes no mention of the Museum having been ruined. It is almost unnecessary to add that the final parallel between Florus and Lucan (*tela hostium submovit* and *populos revocavit ab aula*) must also derive from Livy, and makes it clear that he cannot have regarded the fire as having occurred during a supposed 'sack' of Alexandria.

7

Conjectures

T HE conflict of contradictory opinion about what became of the books of Alexandria has its origins in
our uncertainty about the topography of the Museum.
The discussion has focussed on two questions: a) was the
library a separate building or should we identify it with the
Museum?, and b) was it or was it not within the royal palace?

Both questions, it might be said, are actually easily
resolved, and should perhaps never even have arisen, given
that a) Strabo lists the buildings making up the Museum,
and does not mention a separate library building (XVII,
1, 8); and b) both Strabo, in the passage just cited, and
Tzetzes in his *De comoedia* (Koster's ed., p. 43) clearly
locate the library of the Museum 'inside the palace' (*entos
ton anaktoron*) as opposed to that of the Serapeum, which
was 'outside'. Nonetheless, there has been disagreement
(impossible to resolve by examining the site, since nothing has survived there) because certain of our sources –
Gellius, Plutarch, Ammianus Marcellinus – contain references to a 'fire' in the 'great library'. Once credence is given
to these references (which are in fact of doubtful validity, as

we have argued), it follows that:

a) Since the spread of the fire is very clearly traced in the surviving sources, and since we know that it was started *in* the port and developed *around* the port, attempts have been made (notwithstanding what Strabo and Tzetzes explicitly tell us) to locate the library *near* the port;

b) Since the Museum itself continued in its calmly prosperous existence, and since an unbroken series of literary sources and documents (beginning with Strabo) assure us of its thriving and uninterrupted career, some scholars have come to think that there was a library (which fell victim to the flames) *distinct* from the Museum building.

It was odd, admittedly, if the library caught fire and the Museum did not. Various deliberately obscure references have accordingly been made to the 'distance' between Museum and library. John William White's confusion over the question, for instance, is betrayed by the tortuous phraseology of the essay he wrote as an Introduction to the *Scholia on the Aves of Aristophanes* (London 1914). This is really a history of the library of Alexandria, whose exceptional importance White recognises. Having told us that it was 'probably situated near the Museum, if it was not part of it' (xii), he speaks a little further on of 'the great library connected to the Museum' (xxx).

In fact, Gustav Parthey had long ago indicated the right line of approach. Strabo's topographical descriptions, he pointed out, had proved extremely accurate wherever it had been possible to verify them against on-the-ground evidence. He drew attention to the tendency of eighteenth-century scholars, in particular Bonamy in the

various articles he published in the *Mémoires de l'Académie des Inscriptions et Belles Lettres* of 1731 and 1732, to 'push the library towards the sea' (precisely to make it seem more probable that it might have been burned); and he concluded by emphasising how absurd it was to think that 'the books should have been kept in one building and the scholars should have lived somewhere else' (*Das alexandrinische Museum*, pp. 20–21).

Despite this, modern scholarship has gradually come to adopt the view that the library was quite distinct from the Museum, and was destroyed by a fire that left the Museum unscathed: supposedly, all the sources agree in bearing witness to the library's destruction. This view has been enshrined in works whose authoritative status discourages criticism. It should however be said that it is more firmly established among textual scholars than among archaeologists. The Swedish archaeologist Christian Callmer, for example, whose work on the libraries of antiquity is of unrivalled completeness, remarks cautiously that we actually know nothing of the 'architectural plan' of the library at Alexandria; and he adds a note pointing out that the only surviving description is Strabo's ('Antike Bibliotheken', in *Acta Instituti Romani Regni Suediae*, 1944, p. 148). Carl Wendel, on the other hand, reconstructs the chain of events as follows in the *Handbuch* (III, 1, pp. 75–76):

> When, in the course of the Alexandrian war (48 – 47), Caesar destroyed the enemy ships by fire, this fire also attacked parts

of the city and destroyed the naval yards, the grain warehouses and the great library. As this is a point on which Seneca (following Livy), Dion Cassius, Gellius and Plutarch all agree, one can hardly cast doubt upon it because Caesar himself, in his *Bellum civile,* passes over the painful incident in silence, as does his collaborator, the author of the *Bellum Alexandrinum*; or because later writers such as Orosius or Ammianus Marcellinus confuse the Museum library with the library in the Serapeum. Nor ought one to invoke, against the thesis that there was a fire, the fact that the Museum, being part of the royal palace, was not near the port; and this fact should not be made the basis of unfounded theories such as the hypothesis (advanced by Parthey) that at the relevant time part of the library was being stored in the environs of the port because Caesar was intending to remove it to Rome. We violate the sources if we regard the fire as having taken place not in the library of the Museum but in some other store of books located somewhere else in the city or near the port. The event recorded in the tradition is inherently perfectly possible and we have every reason to accept the soundness of the record.

As we have seen, it may well be objected that neither Seneca, Dion, Gellius, Orosius, nor Ammianus speaks of a fire in the *library* (this word is found only in Plutarch) – they speak of *scrolls* having been burned, giving various figures, from 40,000 to 700,000; that if we seek to explain the silence of both Caesar and the author of the *Bellum Alexandrinum* by their reluctance to record an unpleasant incident, it remains difficult to understand why Cicero (who never mentioned the fire, even after the dictator's death) should have been complicit in this reticence; and that once we have agreed to 'save' the Museum from the flames (even Wendel accepts that it remained intact), it is hard to claim that the library was destroyed without being obliged to remove it to a location elsewhere in the city.

Fraser, the author of the monumental _Ptolemaic Alexandria_ (Oxford 1972), brought some sense into this discussion. A careful student – significantly – of Alexandria's topography, he took the question back to its starting-point: the fact that Strabo nowhere mentions any library building distinct from the other buildings of the Museum. He noted that no such building was to be found at Pergamum, either (where sufficient remains survive for us to be able to reconstruct the ground plan), and that Pergamum must certainly have been based on Alexandria; and he concluded, with his customary caution, that he tended to favour the idea that the so-called 'library' should be understood, in accordance with the first and chief meaning of _bibliothekai_, as consisting of all the bookshelves located in the Museum precincts (I, pp. 334–335; II, pp. 479–480 and 493–494).

Bertrand Hemmerdinger ('Que César n'a pas brûlé la bibliothèque d'Alexandrie', in _Bollettino dei classici_, III, 6, 1985, pp. 76–77) has brought together and commented on the documentary and literary evidence (Papyrus Merton, 19 and Papyrus Oxyrhyncus, 2192; and Suetonius, _Life of Claudius_, 42, 5) which shows that the Museum at Alexandria flourished with no interruption. Therefore, he concludes, there can have been no disastrous loss of books during Caesar's campaign; and he rejects, without discussion, the sources which state that there was.

In fact, although the view stated by Wendel has been the dominant one, dissenting voices have never quite been silenced. Those distancing themselves from the prevailing thesis have included such distinguished authorities on Hellenism and ancient books as Schubart (*Das Buch bei den Griechen und Römern*, 3rd. ed., 1921), Pasquali (see his article 'Biblioteca' in the *Enciclopedia Italiana*, VI, 1930) and Pfeiffer (*History of Classical Scholarship*, Oxford 1968, p. 217). One troublesome point which has cropped up again and again has been the question of how the Museum's scholarly activities could have continued to thrive in the immediate aftermath of the supposed disaster. (Didymus, for example, whose career ended in the Augustan period, had probably already begun work before Caesar's arrival, and would seem to have pressed on without any interruption.) Attempts have been made (for instance, by Wendel) to resolve the puzzle by lending credence to Plutarch's statement that Antony may have given Cleopatra books from Pergamum (*Life* of Antony, 58, 3), even though Plutarch himself says in the following chapter (59) that he does not believe any such gift was made.

Considerable sleight of hand has been lavished on this passage. A notable instance is in White's essay (p. xxx). Calvisius, says Plutarch, libelled Antony by claiming that he had robbed Pergamum of its books in order to give them to Cleopatra; he then remarks that he sets little store by the anecdote. White, citing Plutarch, informs us that Antony gave 200,000 scrolls to Cleopatra, thus restoring the Alexandrian library, and the affair was so scandalous that Calvisius libellously attacked him!

The fact that Wendel, in the passage quoted, adopts a rather polemical tone is explained by the persistence of doubts concerning Caesar's fire. The most passionate defence of the view that no such fire took place (though its passion is not matched by argumentative rigour, and the case is far from conclusively made) will be found in a book by the American classical antiquarian Edward Alexander Parsons (*The Alexandrian Library, Glory of the Hellenistic World*, 1952: see pp. 288–319).

The entire discussion rests on a false basis. It should rightly start from the parallel between Seneca (*De tranquillitate animi*, 9, 5) and the best codices of Orosius, where both give the figure of *forty thousand* scrolls. Instead, Seneca's figure has itself been called in question. White (p. xxxiv, note) disposes of it by speculating that Seneca perhaps set down a number which would have seemed 'sufficiently large', to a Roman of his times, for the stock of a library; in this connection, he has recourse to the peculiar argument that there were many libraries at Rome, but their dimensions were small. Wendel, well aware that Seneca depends on Livy, nonetheless hastens to amend his text – for otherwise, we would end up losing the famous fire in the library. Indeed, 40,000 scrolls, however precious, would not amount to much by comparison with the 490,000 which, so Tzetzes tells us (Koster's ed., p. 43), were already in the library's possession in Callimachus's time.

The truth is that once we have established that Livy, Seneca and Orosius agree on the 'modest' number of 40,000, we can no longer place any trust in the exaggerations of Gellius (and Ammianus after him), according to

which 700,000 scrolls were burned. This hyperbolic figure stands revealed for what it no doubt was, a conjecture
based on the following line of reasoning: a) the library
was destroyed; b) there were 700,000 scrolls in it; c) *ergo*,
700,000 scrolls were burned.

Perhaps the 40,000 scrolls destroyed in the fire, because
they were 'by chance' in storage in the port depots, did
form part of the palace library – either because Caesar had
had them removed there, as Parthey suggests, or for some
other reason unknown to us. Even in that case, they were no
more than a tiny part of the vast collection at Alexandria.

We must agree, then, that the history of the classical
textual tradition never suffered the grave blow that would
have been inflicted by the loss of such a library, had that
loss actually taken place.

Hecataeus

DIODORUS Siculus presents the description of the tomb of Rameses (or Ozymandias) given by Hecataeus of Abdera as *confirming his own direct observation* of the monument (I, 47, 1). Paradoxically, however, he backs up this claim by then giving not his *own* description, but Hecataeus's.

This peculiar device is revealed when we examine the way Diodorus inserts the description into its context. Writing of the monuments of Thebes and its environs, he states:

> Not only what the priests unearth from their records, but also the writings of many of the Greeks – among them Hecataeus – who journeyed as far as Thebes in the days of Ptolemy son of Lagus, *are in accord with the things said by me.*

Hitherto, Diodorus has not 'said' anything, and has not embarked on his description. He now continues by stating that 'he says' – 'he' being Hecataeus! – that

> there is a distance of ten stadia between the mausoleum of the king called Ozymandias and the first tombs where the concubines of Zeus are supposed to be buried; that at the entrance to this mausoleum there is a doorway of worked stone. . . .

This topsy-turvy account reveals that a) at this point, Diodorus begins to copy Hecataeus exactly; b) the mausoleum was still standing when Diodorus visited Thebes; c) Diodorus must have confined himself to reporting what he had found in Hecataeus because he did not actually visit the inside of the mausoleum himself.

The mausoleum of Rameses – the Ramesseum – is the only Theban monument described by Diodorus. His description has become our sole source of information wherever the material remains grow scanty or confused – as, unfortunately, they do when we move beyond the covered walk and into the second part of the building. This is also the point at which Hecataeus's words (quoted by Diodorus) suggest that he was shown no more of the monument, but simply had it described to him (see above, Chapter III).

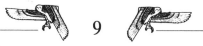

9

The Elusive Library

ARCHAEOLOGISTS have sought in vain for the library of the Ramesseum.

Two officers of the engineers who served in Napoleon's General Staff during his Egyptian campaign, Jean-Baptiste Prosper Jollois and René Edouard Devilliers, first asserted that the mausoleum was the building described by Diodorus, supporting their view with documentary evidence (*Description de l'Egypte*, II, Paris 1821). Although they referred to the building by the old name of 'Memnonion', they were aware that the term was inaccurate. Commendably, they carried out an accurate comparison between Diodorus's description and the remains still visible on the ground. No significant remains, they observed, existed beyond the colonnaded hall; but they nonetheless considered the question of where Diodorus's 'sacred library' (I, 49, 3) should be located. The solution they proposed was somewhat vague. They followed Diodorus in regarding what they called the 'room used as a library' as contiguous with the 'room enclosing twenty tables surrounded by couches' (p. 301), but said that the *oikemata*, the 'small dark chambers', 'surrounded the library' (p. 300), whereas according to

Diodorus they actually surrounded not the library but the room with the twenty couches.

In 1828–1829, a Franco-Tuscan archaeological party undertook an extensive Egyptian expedition. Ippolito Rosellini was among the members of this well-equipped team, led by Jean-François Champollion. As well as confirming that the mausoleum was indeed to be identified with the building described in Diodorus, Champollion attempted to locate the 'room with the books' more precisely. On the doorway between 'the covered walk and the next room', he noticed the figures of two gods carved at the foot of the doorposts. These divinities might well allude to the world of books and reading, being Thoth, the god of knowledge (the Hermes Trismegistus of the Greeks), and his sister Seshat, patron deity of archives (whom Champollion calls 'the goddess Saf, companion of Thoth'). The reliefs also show various members of the two gods' train – among them an associate of Thoth, surmounted by an enormous eye, who represents the sense of sight; and a companion of Seshat, who represents hearing and is not only surmounted by an ear but also carries writing equipment with him 'as if to write down everything he hears'. 'How better than by such bas-reliefs', continued Champollion in the long letter he wrote from Thebes on 18 June 1829, 'could the entrance to a *library* he announced?' Shortly afterwards, however, reconsidering Diodorus's text and comparing it with the surviving ruins of the monument, he stated that 'the room that formed the library is almost entirely razed to the ground' (*Lettres et Journaux*, ed. Hermine Hartleben, Paris 1909, pp. 324, 327).

There have been several subsequent attempts to find some trace of the library inside the mausoleum, or else to locate it more exactly on the basis of Diodorus's description and of such tenuous signs as have survived on the site. Little success has been achieved. At the most, a trace or two has come to light outside the mausoleum. Karl Richard Lepsius, a pupil of Rosellini and the author of *Denkmäler aus Aegypten und Aethiopien* (1849–1859), found to the southwest of Rameses' palace the tombs of two 'librarians', which dated in his view from the time of Rameses II and which he accordingly connected with the library 'described' (as he put it) 'by Diodorus'. Lepsius was thinking in terms of a large and well endowed library such as would indeed have been staffed by librarians. The idea grew more and more prevalent that Diodorus's 'sacred library' had occupied an entire wing of the mausoleum, taking up several rooms; and this notion found its way into successful popular works such as the book on *Egypt* by the Egyptologist and novelist Georg Ebers.

Some years later, J.E. Quibell undertook excavations at Thebes (1895–1896) on behalf of the Egyptian Research Account. He searched the Ramesseum high and low for papyrus remains, and was much disappointed to find only two tiny fragments.

Quibell drew up a new and accurate plan of the Ramesseum (see Figure 4). He distinguished, among other things, between those few walls still standing (indicated by an unbroken line) and those which are conjectural. On the basis of this plan and of a fresh examination of the ruins, Godefroy Goossens offered a more detailed account of the identity and location of the sacred library in the *Chronique d'Egypte* (July 1942, p. 182). He followed Diodorus in writing that 'next there came a covered walk and a number of rooms, which served among other things as kitchens'. The covered walk (*promenoir*) as envisaged by Goossens actually consists of three successive rooms or spaces which he calls 'small hypostyles'.

The first of these contained the relief showing the king offering up the produce of his mines; the second contained the library. Shortly afterwards, however, the first room is referred to as the *promenoir*, and the 'library' is said to comprise both the second and the third room:

> Beyond this walk lay the 'library', the *second* small hypostyle: the place of the cure of the soul *and* a room in which there was a representation of the king making offerings to Osiris and all the gods of Egypt. . . . This room, contiguous with the library [the library is thus identified exclusively with the second room once more], was richly furnished, containing twenty couches. . . .

So this 'contiguous' room is first said to contain the relief showing the pharaoh making offerings to all the gods, and then said to contain the twenty couches – whereas Diodorus

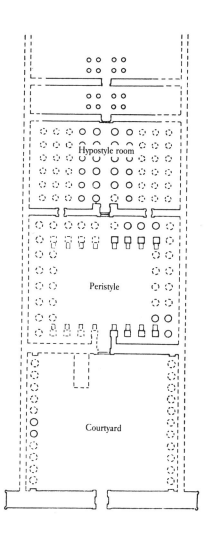

3. The Ramesseum at Thebes: plan, according to Jollois and Devilliers.

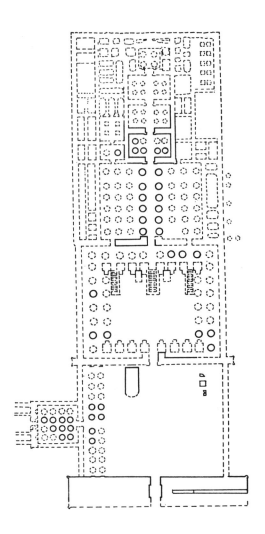

4. Plan of the Ramesseum: Quibell's reconstruction.

quite clearly locates the relief showing the offerings *before* the room with the couches and 'following' the library. The distortion of what Diodorus tells us is all the stranger given that no remains exist of this part of the mausoleum: as Goossens himself notes, 'the last part of the temple is destroyed and it is therefore impossible to relate Diodorus's text to the actual arrangement of the building'.

Nor is this all. In his letter from Thebes (p. 327), Champollion had said that the relief of the pharaoh's offerings to the gods was on the wall that divided the first room from the second – which altogether discredits Goossens' suggestion that it should be located in the same room as the couches (room 3). Champollion also said that there was a relief on the posts of the door into room 2, which would seem to be the picture of the pharaoh offering the products of his mines (this is confirmed by the description given by Goossens, who does indeed locate that relief in the first room). We must ask, then, where on earth the library can have been, given Diodorus's statement that it was *between the two reliefs*. Philippe Derchain ('Le tombeau d'Osymandias', *Nachrichten der Akademie der Wissenschaften zu Göttingen*, 1965, pp. 165–171) has succinctly expressed the view that Diodorus's description of the mausoleum from the covered walk onwards may have been largely imaginary. Diodorus, Derchain argues, derives his account – in whole or in part, it is not clear which – from the imaginative informants who served as his guides when he visited the monument.

What we read must thus be a 'theoretical' description, modelled on a building of some religious significance, the so-called 'house of life' (whose function has been much discussed). Derchain concludes that at all events the sacred library should probably be looked for in one of the side wings of the Ramesseum, and that the 'covered walk' may actually have been an outside corridor. This hypothesis has found few supporters.

A new approach has been adopted by H.W. Helck (in an article in the *Festschrift Jantzen*, Wiesbaden 1969, p. 74) and by Vilmos Wessetzky ('Die ägyptische Tempelbibliothek', *Zeitschrift für ägyptische Sprache und Altertumskunde*, 100, 1973, pp. 54–59). Underlying their suggestions is the notion that the word *peripatos* in Diodorus (I, 49, 1) should in fact be taken to indicate not a place in which people walk (although this would seem to be the sense demanded, since Diodorus writes 'following this is found a *peripatos*') but the 'act of walking'. On this basis, the two scholars speculate that the visitor (Hecataeus) was conducted around the colonnaded hall, forming the impression that he was following a corridor while he was in the space between the columns and the wall; and they further claim that the library should be identified with the small rooms giving off what Champollion, Goossens and many other authorities had regarded as the 'covered walk' (see Figure 5).

Helck (p. 74) offers a bold translation of *sunecheis de tautei*: the reliefs, he writes, were 'within the space reserved for the library'. Mistaken though it is, this translation had already been favoured by Jollois and Devilliers (p. 276) and by Derchain (p. 168). Wessetzky avoids such rashness, and informs the reader that the word *sunecheis* means 'beside' or 'near' rather that 'in', and that the reliefs must accordingly have been *outside*; but he does not draw the necessary inferences so far as the library's topography is concerned.

This thesis has fallen out of favour in its turn. Rainer Stadelmann, the latest scholar to turn his attention to the Ramesseum (see his article 'Ramesseum' in the *Lexikon der Aegyptologie*, V, 1983, pp. 94, 98), offers some thoughts about the small rooms mentioned by Champollion: but these rooms, he acknowledges, have nothing to do with any library (the library, he argues, is to be located back in the first hypostyle); they are, in his view, the usual 'places of sacred embarcation'. The fact that there is no trace of a library had been revealed some years earlier (in 1974) by Jean-Claude Goyon and Hassan El-Achirie, in what may be called the first true publication devoted to the Ramesseum (see the VIth volume, Cairo, 1974, pp. i–iii). The decoration of Room R, Champollion's 'room with the books', was devoted entirely to the depiction of offerings made to the various divinities, and revealed the real function of the room, which clearly had a religious significance and should more properly be called the 'room of litanies'.

The discussion has thus returned to its starting point, but no-one now feels the kind of confidence that made Champollion so sure he had identified the library beyond doubt thanks to the reliefs on the doorposts. Surprisingly little has been made of the fact that the words 'Place of the Cure of the Soul' are not inscribed on this doorway bearing the images of Thoth and Seshat, which supposedly gives entrance to the library. The lack of any such inscription on the surviving ruins has not prevented some scholars, Helck among them, from wondering what Egyptian words actually corresponded to the Greek phrase quoted by Diodorus.

All in all, as Fritz Milkau put it some years ago, 'the library of the Ramesseum is unwilling to be found' (*Handbuch der Bibliothekswissenschaft*, III. 1 [second ed.], 1955, pp. 10–11).

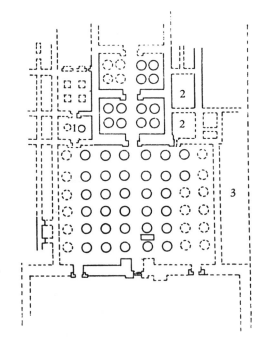

5. *Location of the library in the Ramesseum:* 1, Helck's hypothesis; 2, Wessetzky's hypothesis; 3, the colonnaded hall.

Milkau did not call the existence of the 'sacred library' in doubt; rather, he suggested that it might have been a 'temple library' and that such libraries may well have existed in many temples of the time. He was nonetheless careful to list the shortcomings of previous investigations, and he stated that the small library in the temple of Horus at Edfu (to which we shall turn shortly) was 'the only Egyptian library whose existence there is no justification for doubting'.

Carl Wendel, who was disposed to accept the traditional data, rejected Milkau's cautions and questionings in the article he wrote for the *Reallexikon für Antike und Christentum*. In his summing up of the debate, Wendel argues that the information given by Diodorus 'ought not to be called in question solely because it has proved impossible to establish exactly where the library was in the ruins of the mausoleum at Thebes'. The issue, we may observe, should not be put in these terms. Diodorus's description has been misunderstood (see Chapter XIV above): he refers, not to a library room, but to a 'shelf' (*bibliotheke*) running along the covered walk.

Wendel than goes on to invoke the parallel of the temple of Horus at Edfu:

> It is true that the vestibule of the temple of Horus, which incorporates library fixtures (*Bibliothek-Einbau*), was completed by Ptolemy Euergetes II ('Physkon'). However, the entire Ptolemaic building must have been based on an earlier ancient Egyptian plan. Here, an inscription on the walls of the little room lists two gifts of books made by the king, totalling thirty-seven titles, and *we can see two small recesses in the wall,*

which make it plain that the shelves for the scrolls were inserted here; a representation of Seshat, goddess of writing, offers a final reference to the purpose for which the whole building was intended (II, 1954, col. 232).

Even as he searches for some indication of a library room Wendel thus provides an instance of a *bibliotheke* consisting of a shelf inserted into a niche in the wall.

The location of this *bibliotheke* in the Edfu temple allows us to understand why Diodorus (I, 49, 4) describes the *bibliotheke* in the covered walk of the Ramesseum as 'contiguous' (*homotoichos*) to the room with the triclinia. In the Edfu temple, the two *bibliothekai*, or in other words the two niches in which the shelves used to fit, are carved into the wall that divides the large entrance hall from the succeeding room (see Figure 6, a and b). This dividing wall consists of six inter-columnar spaces closed off with curtain walling that runs halfway up the columns. It is on the inside of this walling that the *bibliothekai* were placed (the two niches which held them being still visible), while the catalogue of scrolls was drawn up on the outside wall (see Hans Wolfgang Müller, 'The Architecture of Ancient Egypt', in the volume by Lloyd, Müller and Martin published in Italian translation as *Architettura mediterranea preromana*, Milan 1972, pp. 172–173). Thus the 'library' of the temple at Edfu is *homotoichos* to the large hypostyle room (to use the term employed by Diodorus in his account of the 'library' of the Ramesseum): *homotoichos* because, precisely, one and the same dividing wall shuts off the hypostyle room and constitutes the wall in which the *bibliothekai* were made. This must be the sense of Diodorus's expression when he

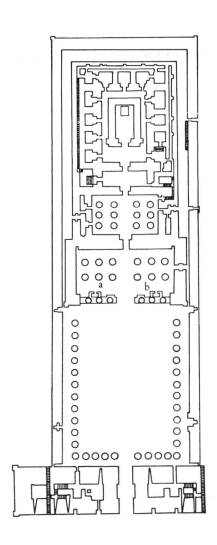

6. Plan of the Temple of Horus at Edfu.

describes the 'sacred library' as being *homotoichos* to the room with the triclinia.

The two 'libraries' in the temple of Horus at Edfu and in the Ramesseum at Thebes must thus have been similar in structure and function – as is consistent with the striking parallels between the two buildings' architecture. Milkau was right to insist on the idea that a 'temple library' (*Tempel-Bibliothek*) usually accompanied a temple. For this very reason, because the books there would basically have consisted of scrolls connected with the cult, vast numbers of scrolls cannot have been involved. Thirty-seven titles are listed near the recess in the temple of Horus, and this gives us an idea of the library's size. This is another reason why we must not imagine that there was a library room, still less a library incorporating several rooms.

The temple of Horus at Edfu was completely rebuilt in the Ptolemaic era, but the original plan is thought to have been retained. It is entirely plausible that the architects of the Ptolemaic royal palace may likewise have followed the model offered by a mausoleum such as the Ramesseum, which incorporated a wing closely resembling the Museum. This would moreover have been in line with the policy of adopting the ways of subject peoples – a policy especially favoured by Alexander, who founded the palace (Diodorus, XVII, 52, 4). What would have been more natural than to imitate the architecture of the pharaohs, and in particular to copy the way they joined together palace, library and *soma*?

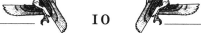

10

The *Soma* of Rameses

THE *Soma* of Rameses is surrounded by an aura of mystery: clearly, its location was a secret. A pharaoh's burial-place was often wrapped in this kind of secrecy. Diodorus notes other examples, for which he mentions various reasons. After describing the human energy and labour spent on the construction of the pyramids, he goes on (I, 64, 4–6) to note that:

> Even though the Kings [Chemnis and Cephren] had had them built as sepulchres for their own use, neither of them was buried there in the end. The people, full of anger because of what they had suffered while they were being built and because of the cruel and violent conduct of these sovereigns, threatened to tear the bodies in pieces and throw them from their tombs with insults and abuse. So they were both buried clandestinely, in a hidden place.

The pharaohs were obsessed with the danger that their tombs might be profaned after their deaths. Diodorus also tells us about the rites performed on the death of the pharaoh, which had clear consequences for the way in which his corpse would be treated. After certain preparatory operations, the body was taken to the entrance of the tomb (these, it is clear, were tombs cut into the rock in the 'valley of the kings'). Here the late ruler's deeds were subject to an 'evaluation' in which all were free to express their criticisms. If the priests' eulogies were felt to be exaggerated or false, those present loudly expressed their disagreement. Diodorus (I, 72, 6) recounts that

it has even happened, in the case of a good number of sovereigns, that the negative opinion expressed by those present at the ceremony has resulted in their being denied an open (*emphanous*) and legitimate burial. And many sovereigns have accordingly chosen to conduct themselves well, partly through fear that on their deaths their corpses might be profaned and they might be branded forever with a verdict of condemnation.

In the case of Rameses, then, we may well wish to preserve the unusual option either of believing what the priests 'revealed' to Hecataeus ('It seems that the king's body had been buried here', in the hall with the triclinia: so Hecataeus, in rather cautious terms, informs us of this 'revelation'), or else of taking note that there is in fact a 'tomb of Rameses', tomb number seven, whose existence we can verify in the valley of the kings.

'It seems that the king's body had been buried here' (*en oi dokein kai to soma tou basileos entethaphthai*): the phraseology need not imply that the pharaoh's body was still there when Hecataeus met the priests. The 'tomb' is referred to immediately afterwards, but in terms which have raised some doubts. Hecataeus says that 'by climbing up through these chambers' – the chambers placed around the hall with the triclinia – one ascended *pros holon ton taphon.*

These words might be rendered 'the sepulchre as a whole'; but it is difficult to know what to make of them. Derchain translates them, obscurely, as 'all the tomb' (p. 167), while Jollois and Devilliers offer the far-fetched gloss 'the place which is really built as a tomb' (p. 277). Hertlein suggested that the correct reading was not *pros holon* but *pros akron*, and translated: 'towards the summit of the sepulchre'.

However, the overall sense of the description is clear. The funerary monument was on the roof of the hall with the triclinia (as also was the golden circle). The way up was along a ramp that ran through the chambers giving off the hall. The temple of Hathor at Denderah offers an example, still well preserved, of a small kiosk placed on the roof and accessible by two ramps or flights of stairs. The so-called 'labyrinth' near lake Moeris, described several times in sources both Greek (Herodotus, Diodorus, Strabo) and Roman (Pliny, Pomponius Mela), is another celebrated instance. Here, one had to 'climb onto the roof' (Strabo XVII, 1, 37 has *anabanta epi to stegos*) before making one's way through a series of rooms and so reaching 'a pyramid-shaped construction with a quadrangular base, which was in fact the funerary monument' of the sovereign (whom Strabo calls by the generic name Ismandes, equivalent either to Memnon or to Ozymandias). Diodorus also speaks, briefly, of this monument (I, 61 and 66). Herodotus (II, 148) was the original model: he claimed to have direct knowledge of much of the building, and said that there were thousands of rooms. Here again we find contradictory information about the real whereabouts of the tomb. According to Strabo, it was in the pyramid: but Herodotus was told that 'the sovereigns and sacred crocodiles' were buried in subterranean rooms, for which reason it was not possible to gain access to them.

Herodotus, in his necessarily condensed description, speaks of halls, doorways and atria succeeding one another interminably. Here, too, the halls were roofed with stone, the inner walls were covered with figures, and columns ran around each atrium. The underlying model – employed, in the building near lake Moeris, on a dizzying scale – is the same: here as in the Ramesseum, the repetition of identical rooms disorients and deceives the visitor. Both buildings are indeed labyrinths, the function of which is, among other things, to conceal the sovereign's mummified corpse.

THE PLACE OF THE CURE OF THE SOUL

The *Ka* is the 'vital force' – the 'soul', one might say – of the sovereign, a 'force' with which the gods, and a few chosen mortals, are endowed. In Egyptian religious thought, its task was to preserve the pharaoh alive after his death (see P. Kaplony, article on *Ka* in the *Lexikon der Aegyptologie*, III, 1980, col. 276). Egyptian funerary mausolea generally contain a place set apart for it, closely connected with the *sancta sanctorum*. In the Ramesseum, the dwelling-place of the *Ka* was probably in the hall with the triclinia.

This can be inferred from the much-discussed inscription *psyches iatreion*. If *iatreion* means (see *Thesaurus Graecae Linguae*) *officina medici, locus ubi medicus artem suam exercet* ('the workshop of a physican, the place where a physician practises his art'), and if *psyche* is a translation of *Ka,* then we may well conclude that the phrase *psyches iatreion* denotes, precisely, the dwelling or (better) the 'workshop', where the *Ka* resides and where it operates.

If, moreover, the wall with the bookshelves in the Ramesseum opened into the hall with triclinia, then the inscription *psyches iatreion* should be taken to designate not the shelf below, but the room the visitor was about to enter: the hall with the triclinia, which was the *officina* or 'workshop' of the *Ka.* The 'soul' referred to is Rameses' *Ka.* Scholars have been mistaken in taking the inscription as an allusion to the benefit the human soul can derive from the reading of good books, an anachronistic interpretation consistent with their belief that the Ramesseum contained a library room with these words above its entrance.

In the dwelling of the *Ka* (Maspéro called it the *maison de l'âme,* the house of the soul), there was usually a statue representing the dead king. Diodorus, who tells us that such a statue was indeed found in the hall with the triclinia, was not speaking at random when he added: 'It seems that the king's body had been buried here.'

11

Kadesh

I T is hard to believe that the priests who accompanied
Hecataeus when he visited the Ramesseum really
mentioned the rebellion in Bactria when they came to the
bas-relief of the battle of Kadesh (Diodorus, I, 47, 6).
After all, the accompanying explanatory inscriptions made
it even easier to identify the scene shown in the relief.
Jacoby, in his collection of Hecataeus's literary remains,
pointed out the problems involved in the reference to the
Bactrians (*Die Fragmente der griechischen Historiker*, No. 264,
F. 25: p. 33, I. 32).

Rameses II's victory over the Hittites was indeed a
famous one. It took place in the fifth year of his reign
(and can be dated, according to the calculations of Eduard
Meyer, *Geschichte des Altertums*, II, 1, Berlin 1928, p. 462,
to 16 May of 1294 BC; an alternative and more recent
date has also been put forward). It was the most crucial
military event not just of Rameses' reign but perhaps of
the entire 'new dynasty'. It is celebrated in the so-called
'Iliad of Egypt' attributed to Pentaur, the scribe whose name
appears at the foot of the text. In the poem, the Pharaoh, at
a critical moment of the battle, says: 'I found myself alone,

and nobody was with me'. Rameses had this phrase cut over
and over again on the architrave of the temple of Ammon.
The turning-points of the battle are represented, in obses-
sive repetition, in every one of the temples built for him
(Meyer, pp. 460–461): not just the Ramesseum, but Abu-
Simbel, Luxor, Abydos, and elsewhere (Meyer, p. 502,
calculated that at least six depictions of the scene have
survived). The rock temple of Abu Simbel is of particular
interest, for here the images of the defeated enemy are
accompanied by detailed commentaries whose phraseology
is partially echoed in the relief in the Ramesseum (Meyer,
p. 460, note 2). The temple of Rameses at Luxor carefully
distinguishes, among the peoples shown, no less than twelve
types or races (Semites, Bedouins, Hittites and so forth),
all of them overcome by the invincible force of Rameses'
arms.

None of this, of course, obliges us to believe the hyper-
bolical boasts of the XIX dynasty pharaohs, who claimed that
their dominions extended as far as India and Bactria. The
texts which relate this claim are not altogether clear. They
are of roughly the same date, and derive from the Egyptian
visits made by Strabo (25–20 BC) and Germanicus (19
AD). The relevant passage in Strabo follows immediately
after his description of the Memnonion, with its remarkable acoustic properties, which he tentatively suggests may
involve trickery of some kind. He then writes that 'above
the Memnonion are the tombs of the kings, carved out in
caves, some forty in number, wonderfully constructed and
deserving to be seen' (XVII, 1, 46: this is the 'valley of the
kings', with its fifty-eight tombs). What follows is unclear:

the manuscripts read *en de tais thekais,* 'in the tombs', and
the passage continues

> on certain obelisks, there are inscriptions proclaiming the
> wealth of the sovereigns of the time and the extent of their
> dominions – as far as the Scythians, Bactrians and Indians,
> and encompassing what is now Ionia; and the amount of tribute
> they received and the size of their armies, which numbered as
> many as a million men.

Joergen Zoega, the Danish archaeologist who settled in
Rome shortly before Napoleon's whirlwind descent, proposed in his *De origine et usu obeliscorum* (dated 1797: see
p. 169) that *thekais* ('in the tombs') should be altered to
Thebais ('in Thebes'). Zoega here adopts a suggestion made
by the humanist Antonio Mancinelli. It is difficult to see
how an obelisk 23 metres high (this is the size of Rameses
II's obelisk, which has stood since 1833 in the Place de la
Concorde in Paris) could have been erected in a rock-tomb.
In their editions of Strabo, in 1844 and 1852 respectively,
both Kramer and Meineke adopted the new reading, which
has its basis in the fact that Greek *beta* and *kappa* are almost
inevitably confused with each other in the small lettering of
the ninth and tenth centuries.

But if Strabo locates the obelisks simply 'in Thebes', and
they have nothing to do with the royal tombs, we have to
ask who are the 'sovereigns of the time' referred to in the
inscriptions. There is in fact a whole series of Ptolemaic
inscriptions, often written in hieroglyphic characters as well
as in Greek, whose content exactly parallels what Strabo
describes, for they give a similarly implausible account of

the boundless dominions ruled over by the Ptolemies. One example, from a rather peripheral location, is the so-called 'inscription of Adulis' of Ptolemy III Euergetes (which has come down to us by way of the transcription made in the sixth century AD by Cosmas Indicopleustes: see *Orientis Graeci Inscriptiones Selectae*, ed. Wilhelm Dittenberger, I, no. 54, pp. 86–87). In this official text, Ptolemy states that his dominions embraced

> all the lands on this side of the Euphrates: Caelicia, Pamphilia, Ionia, the Hellespont, Thrace. . . . After he had conquered all the monarchs of these regions, he crossed the Euphrates and made his way through Mesopotamia, Babylon, Susia, Persia and Media, and he brought all the rest as far as Bactria under his own dominion, and brought back to Egypt everything that the Persians had looted.

There is, of course, no historical confirmation for any of this. Dittenberger, using an expression of Mahaffy's (*The Empire of the Ptolemies*, p. 126), describes the passage as *laudes tralaticiae*, 'common and customary praise', and indeed very similar statements are made, in whole or in part, about each of Euergetes' two predecessors. There is even a hieroglyphic inscription, dating from 310 BC, which refers to the first Ptolemy before he had actually been accorded the official title of king and claims, among other things, that he brought back from Persia to Egypt all the statues and sacred books which the Persians had looted (the inscription's text is in H. Brugsch's contribution to the *Zeitschrift für aegyptische Sprache*, 9, 1871, p. 1). This restitution, one notes with some amusement, is attributed to each new sovereign in turn. Ptolemy Euergetes again claims credit for it in the Tanis inscription, known as the *monumentum Canopium*, which is also bilingual (see *Orientis Graeci Inscriptiones Selectae*, no. 56, p. 99).

We must obviously bear in mind that the Egyptian temples were indeed rebuilt (the well-known example of the temple of Horus at Edfu has already been discussed). This must have led to a new Ptolemaic surface being overlaid on the ancient Egyptian substructure: one case in point is the sanctuary of Alexander the Great in the temple of Luxor. This helps explain how the figure of the mythical pharaoh Sesostris (whose identity was the subject of various speculations) came to be in some sense assimilated to that of Alexander: Sesostris, Diodorus tells us, 'occupied not only all those lands which Alexander the Great ruled over, but also nations on whose territory Alexander had never set foot' (I, 55, 3). The practice of laying boastful claim to a kingdom infinitely larger than they actually governed was another legacy the Ptolemies inherited from the pharaohs who had preceded them (A. Wiedemann, *Aegyptische Geschichte,*Gotha 1884, p. 29).

The tediously lengthy *monumentum Canopium* also informs us what sort of crown we should envisage on the head of statues of Berenice, famous for her beautiful hair: it would be 'quite different', we are told, 'from the kind used in statues of [Ptolemy's] mother' (*Orientis Graeci Inscriptiones Selectae*, no. 56, lines 61–62). One thinks at once of the triple crown on the head of Rameses II's mother in the Ramesseum (Diodorus, I, 47, 5). All in all, the Ptolemies clearly came to identify themselves with the modes and ideas of royal sovereignty current among the pharaohs. The link between the plan of the Museum and that of the Ramesseum is a further mark of this identification.

Germanicus was given an account, by an elderly Egyptian priest, which has many parallels with Strabo's. Moreover, the priest mentions the name 'Rameses':

> He then visited the great ruins of the ancient city of Thebes, where the massive buildings still bore hieroglyphs with their message of bygone grandeur. An Egyptian priest, asked to translate the language of his forebears, explained these inscriptions. They stated that seven hundred thousand men fit to bear arms used to live there, and that with this army king Rameses had seized possession of Libya, Ethiopia, Media, Persia, Bactria and Scythia, as well as of the lands of the Syrians, the Armenians and their neighbours the Cappadocians; and that the same king had controlled the sea of Bithynia on one hand and the sea of Lycia on the other. These inscriptions also related what tributes were levied on the peoples and what quantities every nation had to pay in gold and silver, how many arms and horses and temple gifts, how much ivory and perfume, what amount of grain and of the other necessities of life; and the quantities were no less than is now demanded by the might of the Parthians or the power of Rome (Tacitus, *Annals*, II, 60).

Germanicus's guide, a latter-day representative of the old priestly wisdom, used the name 'Rameses' simply to give his account a more authentic flavour (see F.R.D. Goodyear,

The Annals of Tacitus, II, Cambridge 1981, p. 383). Manetho, confused as ever, had identified Rameses II with the mythical Sesostris, a point noted in Tacitus's day by Flavius Josephus in his polemical essay *Contra Apion* (I,98). Sesostris, as we know, had been credited with conquests greater even than those of Alexander (Diodorus, I, 55, 3). But now scholars had come to proceed with greater circumspection, and were cautious in identifying remote and sometimes nebulous sovereigns: 'If Ismandes is Memnon,' writes Strabo (XVII, 1, 42), 'then the Memnonion is his work, as also are the temples of Abydos and Thebes.' Hecataeus's informants, roughly contemporary with Manetho, may already have been quite confused about this difficult subject; at the best, they can only have been priests of Manetho's own type. All the same, it is difficult to understand how historical accounts of the battle of Kadesh can have been so entirely lost or distorted that the engagement came to be located in Bactria, in far-off Afghanistan, one of the limits beyond which Alexander never ventured.

12

Strabo and Neleus

OUR reconstruction of the fate of the Aristotelian texts (see above, Chapters VI and X) involves an implicit judgement on the detailed account given by Strabo (xii, 1, 54). When he tells us how the learned Tyrannion gained possession of Apellicon's original manuscripts (by 'paying court' to Sulla's librarian), Strabo must be relating what he had been told by Tyrannion himself, whose pupil he was. (This is Carl Wendel's conclusion: he refers briefly to the topic in his article on Tyrannion for the 'Pauly-Wissowa' *Encyclopaedia*, col. 1813, 42). Strabo came to Rome in 44 BC, when he was twenty years old. He was from Amasia, and was thus a compatriot of Tyrannion, who came from Amisus. Strabo was probably also echoing Tyrannion in his strongly negative assessment of the work of the copyists employed by Roman booksellers to make 'copies for sale' ('they had not even taken the trouble to collate the texts'); his scathing dismissal of the editorial labours of Apellicon (very few people are likely to have known Apellicon's edition, which was prepared before 86 BC); and his more general condemnation of the copying done for booksellers both in Rome and in Alexandria. Tyrannion was familiar – at any rate at second hand – with Alexandrian books and learning by way of his master, Dionysius of Thrace, who had attended the school of Aristarchus. Perhaps Tyrannion was also responsible for what may be a satirical comment on the deterioration of Apellicon's scrolls once they had reached Rome: the statement that 'Rome, too, lent a helping hand' may well be ironical.

The question of whether and how far we should trust Strabo's account is notoriously controversial. Those who regard Strabo as reliable are entitled to claim in their favour the fact that Tyrannion would seem to have been his informant. Further support comes from Posidonius, who refers (*apud* Athenaeus, V, 214d) to the acquisition by Apellicon of 'Aristotle's library': this authoritatively confirms one of the essential details of Strabo's narrative. Posidonius is a most important witness, both because he was a contemporary familiar with the cultural circle in which Neleus's scrolls ended up and because of his professional interest in the vicissitudes of such an important philosophical collection. In this regard, Plutarch's testimony (*Life of Sulla*, 26) is also valuable and significant, for we should not forget that Plutarch was a scholar directly acquainted with much post-Aristotelian philosophical work, recent and not so recent—work, one assumes, which must surely have contained references to the episode, whose consequences for the development of Greek thought after Aristotle were considerable.

Another and probably independent piece of evidence about Apellicon's role is found in the Arabic list of Aristotle's works said to have been made by 'Ptolemy the

Philosopher'. Ibn al-Kifti reproduces this, with titles and headings in both Arabic and Greek, in his *History of Wise Men*. The best edition of Ibn al-Kifti's text is found in Ingemar Düring's essay on *Aristotle in the Ancient Biographical Tradition* (Göteborg 1957, pp.21–231). Number 92 in his list is followed by the heading: 'Here are the books that were found in the library of a man called Apellicon (*Ablikun*)'.

Two other lists of Aristotle's works have come down to us. One is quoted by Diogenes Laertius (V, 22–27), and the other is in the form of an addendum to the so-called *Vita Menagiana* (Düring, pp. 81–89).

The only explicit information we have about the origin of these lists is in Plutarch's *Life of Sulla* (Chapter 26). Plutarch says that the Aristotelian works which reached Rome as part of Sulla's booty were eventually edited by Andronicus of Rhodes, who also 'drew up the catalogues now current'. Porphyrius (*Life of Plotinus*, 24) tells us that Andronicus 'divided into treatises (*eis pragmateias*) the works of Aristotle and Theophrastus, bringing together related subjects in the same place'. This is a type of work very similar to the making of catalogues. Porphyrius draws a comparison between his own labours on Plotinus and those of Andronicus on Aristotle:

> And in the same way I too, with fifty-four books of Plotinus at my disposal, divided them into six enneads, well pleased that I was able to attain both the ninefoldness of the ennead and the perfection of the number six: and to each ennead I ascribed its own sphere of arguments, gathering these

together and putting the easiest questions in first place. The first ennead in fact contains the following writings. . . . The second ennead brings together treatises on physics etc. . . .

Here we see the close connection between the thematic ordering of books and the drawing up of a catalogue.

Since Plutarch, some hundred years after Andronicus, speaks of the latter's catalogues as being in 'current' use, we can hardly doubt that the surviving lists, in the form in which they have come down to us, must derive to some extent from Andronicus, or must at all events echo his catalogues to a significant degree. This probably applies above all to Ptolemy's list, as Paul Moraux showed in his essay on *Les listes anciennes des ouvrages d'Aristote* (1951). Moraux stresses the differences between the lists, suggesting that Diogenes' compilation and the addendum to the *Vita Menagiana* share a common origin in Ariston, while Ptolemy is closer to Andronicus.

Lists, of course, are difficult texts for the critic, since they are uniquely susceptible to addition or abridgement. It is no coincidence that the three surviving Aristotelian lists differ from one another above all in their length. The addendum to the *Vita Menagiana,* thought to be derived directly from the inventory made by Esychius of Miletus in the 6th century AD, includes, for instance, an appendix, not present in Diogenes, which records a number of treatises (including the *Metaphysics*). Moraux nonetheless claims to show that a lacuna exists in Diogenes' catalogue which can be filled, precisely, by adding the title of the *Metaphysics*. These considerations evidently limit the scope of Moraux's arguments when he attempts (pp. 243–247) to demonstrate that the first two lists both derive from the work of Ariston of Chios, scholarch of the Lyceum at the end of the third century.

The inferences Moraux drew from this hypothesis are obvious. If the lists in Diogenes and the *Vita Menagiana* can indeed be traced back to Ariston, then we can no longer hold that the acroamatic treatises – the orally communicated teachings, of which the *Metaphysics* is one – remained inaccessible for a long period: and this undermines the credibility of Strabo's narrative. If, however, without undervaluing Ariston's contribution, we take the view that the textual arrangement made by Andronicus of Rhodes established itself (as Plutarch states it did) because he was able to take advantage of the 're-emergence' of certain Aristotelian texts, then Strabo's account loses none of its plausibility.

We should in any case observe the general caution against assuming that works were *in fact* available just because lists which included their titles were in circulation. Lists of titles can be conscientiously, and mechanically, handed down irrespective of whether the works in question have been preserved – can be handed down, then, in the *absence* of their preservation. One case among many is provided by Diogenes Laertius himself, who gives impressive lists relating to Theophrastus (V, 42–50) and Democritus (IX, 46–49). Diogenes copied these from his sources: the works referred to, meanwhile, had probably disappeared either totally (in the case of Democritus, they had certainly done so some time earlier) or in part. The same point can be made about the copyists who transmitted Diogenes' work during the Middle Ages, and one can imagine that the situation was similar in antiquity. In the particular case of the lists of Aristotelian works, there can be no doubt that by the time Neleus left for Scepsis with his books – indeed, earlier than this – the Academy must have possessed an inventory of all the relevant material. Lists of this kind, needed in the school, may well have led to the making of catalogues which did not necessarily reflect the actual availability of the works.

The piece of evidence which seems to weigh most heavily against Strabo is found in the opening pages of Athenaeus's _Deipnosophists._ Unfortunately, we do not have Athenaeus's unabridged text for this portion of the work, and must rely on an abstract which is thought to involve a reduction of some forty per cent as compared with the original. Athenaeus recounts the memorable conversations that took place in the house of his patron Livius Larensis, a member of the equestrian order at Rome, and he hastens to describe the extraordinary library which was the greatest distinction of this very rich Roman. It was 'stocked with old Greek books', writes Athenaeus, 'in greater numbers than were possessed by those most admired for the quantity of their books'. He then lists these celebrated library-owners (I, 3A):

> Polycrates of Samos and Pisistratus, tyrant of Athens; Euclid, also of Athens; Nicocrates of Cyprus, and also the king of

Pergamum, the poet Euripides, the philosopher Aristotle, and Theophrastus and Neleus, who looked after their books: it was from this Neleus that my king, Ptolemy called Philadelphus, acquired all his books, transferring them to Alexandria, the beautiful, along with those which came from Athens and Rhodes.

Moraux has commented that 'here Athenaeus is speaking of people who collected books and owned large libraries' and that 'in this context the information that Neleus sold Aristotle's books must be taken to refer to the books Aristotle acquired for his library', and not necessarily to books that he had written (*Der Aristotelismus bei den Griechen*, I, Berlin 1973, p. 13, note 29). Athenaeus's remark, as interpreted by Moraux, underlies the account given in Chapter VI above, where Neleus is said to have played a trick on Ptolemy's messengers by selling them 'Aristotle's books' – the books that made up his library.

Moraux continues as follows (pp. 13–16):

It would certainly seem that Neleus chiefly sold Philadelphus non-Aristotelian books, books collected by Aristotle and Theophrastus. We do not know whether copies of the works of the two philosophers were also included. We know only that works by Aristotle did figure among the books that Neleus kept for himself. It is plausible that Neleus may have withheld certain of Aristotle's writings from the acquisitive grasp of the Alexandrian collectors.

He sums up his views in the claim that:

Half a century after Aristotle's death, at least four cities of the Greek world possessed the philosopher's doctrinal writings:

Scepsis in Troas, Alexandria, Rhodes (where the tradition established by Eudemus was carried on), and certainly also Athens, for it is quite unimaginable that the Academy, following the departure of Neleus, should have had no copies of Aristotle's most important writings.

It is worth noting that when Moraux mentions the Aristotelian writings that can be seen to have left traces in the work of Alexandrian scholars, he actually lists – apart from extracts from zoological writings, taken from Aristophanes of Byzantium – the *Lists of Olympic Victors*, the *Didascalia*, the *Politics*, (and with some doubts) the *Poetics* (p. 15, n. 36). This does not amount to much by comparison with the corpus of orally communicated works.

In considering this nice question (on which no light has been cast by the very defective papyrus text of Philodemus's *Adversus sophistas*), we must not lose sight of the explicit statements of Strabo/Tyrannion and Plutarch, for these are primary sources. Both authors tell us that Neleus's defection seriously damaged the development of the Aristotelian school, and relate the intellectual stagnation that set in there to the fact that after Neleus's unlooked-for departure the philosophical labours of the peripatetics suffered from excessive generality.

The Hellenistic conception of Aristotle's thought was formed above all by the dialogues (as Bignone shows) and, indirectly, by way of Theophrastus (H. Flashar, *Die Philosophie der Antike*, III, Basel 1983, p. 191). Redactions and refashionings of the most important treatises certainly circulated in the Hellenistic period: we can imagine the manner in which they were compiled on the basis of the

traditions of the Aristotelian school. They were super-
seded by Andronicus's critical edition (and the same fate
must have befallen the Athenian edition prepared by the
unfortunate Apellicon, as well as the Roman pirate texts
against which Tyrannion had inveighed). This explains
why it was only in the middle of the second century
AD – with the work of Aspasius, Atticus and Alexander
of Aphrodisia – that creative study and interpretation of
Aristotle began to revive. This rebirth must have been
based on a definitive new edition – the edition made
by Andronicus (see O. Gigon, 'Cicero und Aristoteles',
Hermes, 1959, p. 144).

This is corroborated by what we find in Cicero, whose
work, taken as a whole, reveals an acquaintance only with
the Aristotle of the dialogues. In the *De finibus*, however, written in the first months of 45 AD, the develop-
ing argument of the fifth book is interrupted by a brief,
scholastic exposition of the ethical thought of Aristotle
and Theophrastus (V, 9–14). The argument is not much
to the point: one agrees with Madvig when he remarks in
his commentary on the *De finibus* (Copenhagen, 1838 and
1876 [3rd. ed.], p. 839) *quam non apte et quam inutiliter
interponatur*: 'how inappositely and to what little purpose it
is interposed'. It is here that we find the earliest surviving
reference to the *Nicomachean Ethics*, which Cicero regards
as probably the work of Aristotle's son Nicomachus (*non
video cur non potuerit patri similis esse filius*: 'I do not see
why the son may not have resembled the father'). This is
another indication that the tradition was not as yet firmly
established.

Strabo's account, then, is well founded despite the scepticism which has cast doubt on it. It appears to be based on excellent information, supplied by a source conversant with the history and technical terminology of books and libraries. If, bearing this in mind, we conclude our discussion by looking again at the opening of his narrative, we see that Strabo chooses his words with precision: Neleus, we are told – the allusion is to the clause in the will cited by Diogenes – 'had inherited the *library* of Theophrastus in which that of Aristotle was also included'. From Athenaeus (I, 3A) we know that Neleus did indeed find himself owner of the two great scholarchs' 'personal libraries', composed to a large extent of books they had *acquired*. This is the situation reflected in Strabo's carefully chosen words.

If Theophrastus's library contained Aristotle's library, and the library of Neleus (heir presumptive to the position of Scholarch) contained them both, like Chinese boxes, then we can infer that it was usual for each scholarch to bequeath his books *personally* to his successor. When the Aristotelian 'model' was transplanted to Alexandria, where the Ptolemies had revived the culture of the Pharaohs, the sovereign replaced the scholarch in this respect, and the books became 'the king's books'.

13

Library Traditions

G ELLIUS'S brief narrative, even shorn of its concluding passage (which may have been added by
another hand at a later date), remains a fine example of
the fantasies and learned inventions which the subject of
libraries so readily evokes. Gellius accepts the story that
there had been a public library in Athens in very early times.
This was supposed to have been founded by Pisistratus (a
development of the tradition that Pisistratus had collected
the Homeric books); to have grown larger in subsequent
years; and to have been pillaged and taken off to Persia by
Xerxes, and restored to Athens by Seleucus – who, having
succeeded Xerxes (two hundred years later) on the throne
of Babylon, was evidently obliged to right the wrongs done
by his predecessor. Admittedly, the picture of Seleucus that
came down in Armenian tradition to Mar Ibas (who lived
during the second century BC) was rather different. When
he became king, says Mar Ibas, Seleucus 'had all the books
in the world burned, because he wanted the calculation of
time to begin with himself'.

It must have seemed strange beyond belief that such a
city as Athens should have been without a public library

for a long period. It is nonetheless the case that the city's first public library did not open until a late date. It was established on the initiative of Ptolemy Philadelphus (285–246 BC), who founded in Athens a gymnasium (the 'Ptolemaion') equipped with a library. During the first century BC, the practice developed of adding one hundred scrolls, donated by the ephebes (young citizens), to this library's collection each year. However, the great Athenian library was the one donated to the city by the emperor Hadrian (117–138 AD). This was built around a covered walk which had some one hundred columns, and it included rooms for teaching.

It is as compensation for this actual historical 'backwardness' that the idea of 'the library at Athens' springs up every now and again in our source documents. The seed of the tradition lies in the claim that Pisistratus had collected the Homeric books – just as the first Hebrew 'library' was ascribed to Esdras, who had copied the Old Testament. References to a library existing at Athens in later periods are rare, if not indeed non-existent. In his *Life* of Demosthenes, the scholar whom we know as Zosimus of Ashkelon (or Gaza), who lived in either the fifth or the sixth century AD, speaks of a 'library of Athens' in the days of the great orator (born a century before Ptolemy Philadelphus came to the throne). He does so in connection with an extraordinary feat supposedly performed by Demosthenes. It is not clear when this is meant to have happened – perhaps in his youth – but Zosimus relates that the library of Athens went up in flames, destroying Thucydides' *History*, and that Demosthenes, who remembered the entire work from beginning to end, was able to dictate it, allowing a new copy to be made of the precious text (see *Oratores Attici*, ed. C. Müller, II, p. 523).

Other fantastic elements, inspired by the example of the Alexandrian Museum, further embellished the traditional story that there had been a library in the far-off days of Pisistratus. It is remarkable that such a scholar as Bouché-Leclerc should have accepted the validity of these traditions, writing that 'the Athenians never sought, even in Pericles's time, to reestablish the library founded by the Pisistratidae and stolen by Xerxes. It was restored to the city by Seleucus Nicator' (*Histoire des Lagides*, I, Paris 1903, p. 129). Wendel, too, states in the *Handbuch der Bibliothekswissenschaft* (III, 1 [2nd ed.], p. 55) that 'Seleucus appears to have compensated the Athenians for the damage done by Xerxes by presenting them with books'. It was said that Pisistratus had had collaborators, who studied texts and carried out the 'revision' (*diorthosis*) of the Homeric poems in the manner of such later savants as Zenodotus and Aristarchus. John Tzetzes, the whimsical grammarian who lived a life of poverty in the days of the Comneni, found these details in the source from which he drew his bibliographical data on the Museum and the Serapeum. Indeed, Tzetzes actually gives the names of the four *diorthotai* supposed to have assisted Pisistratus: Orpheus of Croton, Zopyrus of Heraclea, Onomacritus of Athens, and a certain Epicongylus (in this last case the reading is doubtful). This tradition about Pisistratus and his library of course follows the pattern of rivalry between tyrants, and can be seen as an assertion of Athenian prestige

in response to the traditional stories about the library of
Polycrates of Samos.

In his source, Tzetzes also found data on the size
of the Museum and Serapeum collections in the time
of Callimachus; on the Alexandrian librarians (he was
aware, for instance, that Eratosthenes, not Callimachus,
had been librarian); on the tasks allotted to various scholars (Lycophron had edited the comedians, Alexander of
Aetolia the tragedians); and on the systematic programme
of translations into Greek of 'the books of all peoples',
including the Old Testament. It is worth noting that some
of the details – Pisistratus's library; the royal mania for
making Greek versions of the 'books of various peoples'
(*volumina diversarum gentium*); Philadelphus's especial zeal
in such projects, and his initiative in arranging for translations that would include 'sacred writings' (*divinas litteras*)
– can be found five centuries before Tzetzes, in Isidore
of Seville's chapter *de bibliothecis* (IV, 3), discussed above.
Isidore, it will be recalled, then devotes a chapter to these
translations, which contains a brief and undoubtedly in-
direct reflection of Aristeas' account of the correspon-
dence between Ptolemy and Eleazar about the dispatch of
translators of Jerusalem.

Indeed, Aristeas' *Letter* is part of the tradition we are
discussing, for it too is a book 'on libraries'. Although its
author pretends to be relating events of his own time, the
work can date from no earlier than the second century
BC. Aristeas follows the tradition known to Tzetzes in his
unlikely claim that Demetrius Phalereus was connected
with Ptolemy Philadelphus; but he differs when it comes

to figures. Tzetzes sets the Museum's collection at 400,000 *symmigeis* scrolls (scrolls forming part of the works in several scrolls) and 90,000 *amigeis* scrolls (so-called *monobibloi*, in which a single scroll contains the entire work). Aristeas, however, states that the library's stock comprised 200,000 scrolls, and that the 'objective', set by Philadelphus in person, was some 500,000. Gellius and Ammianus, we may infer, arrived at the huge total of 700,000 by adding together these two figures given by Aristeas.

As well as an account of the fire started by Caesar (which he mistakenly locates in the Serapeum), Ammianus (XXII, 16, 15–22) gives us a digression about Alexandria, much of it devoted to the learned men who were the glory of the Museum there. We see here a series of interlinked treatises, a veritable vulgate, 'on libraries'. Within this, facts and myths are mingled, and high figures alternate with low ones. (It is remarkable that Isidore should say that there are just 70,000 scrolls, a figure found also in several codices of Gellius, VII, 17, 3; and that Epiphanius and Ibn al-Kifti should put the Museum's stock of books as low as 54,000 scrolls.) This tradition, which often refers proudly to the far-off precedent established by Pisistratus, came to absorb the essential elements of Aristeas' narrative. For this reason, and also because after a certain date it invariably connected the discussion of 'libraries' with that of 'the translation of the Old Testament' (a striking example is Epiphanius's *Realencyclopädie*), I regard it as being based not on Varro but on a Judaeo-Hellenistic tradition.

In the above interpretation, I have departed from the customary usage of the two well-known terms (*symmigeis* and *amigeis*) used in classifying scrolls. Two hypotheses have held the field hitherto. According to the first, the terms should be rendered 'unsorted scrolls' and 'selected scrolls' (F. Ritschl, *Die Alexandrinischen Bibliotheken*, 1838, pp. 3–4; in *Opuscula*, I, pp. 5–6). According to the second, they mean 'miscellaneous scrolls' and *monobibloi* (Bernhardy, Schneidewein, Birt, Dziatzko and others: this is the current view). Various objections can be made against Ritschl's hypothesis, including the fact that the 200,000 scrolls at Pergamum – all of them, if we accept what Plutarch writes in his *Life of Antony* (58), *amigeis* – seem too many, being more than double the 'selected scrolls' of Alexandria. The prevailing view, on the other hand, is open to the objection that it seems unlikely that 'miscellaneous' scrolls should have constituted a decisive majority of the Alexandrian collection; and to the still stronger objection that the very notion of a 'miscellaneous' scroll is inherently quite implausible (see A. Petrucci, 'Dal libro unitario al libro miscellaneo', in *Tradizione dei classici, transformazioni della cultura*, ed. A. Giardina, Rome-Bari 1986, p. 16).

The true contrary of *monobiblos* (*amiges*) is, precisely, not a 'miscellaneous' scroll but a scroll which together with other scrolls makes up a single work. Most works in fact occupy more than one scroll – hence the disproportion between the two figures, 400,000 and 90,000. Besides, the term *symmiges*, when not applied to books, has the sense 'which unites or joins with others; which is confused or mixed with others'.

For librarians, the scroll was the 'unit of measurement'. This is why we find such large figures in the sources: hundreds of thousands of scrolls – figures less impressive than they seem at first glance, for they derive from the practice of counting not works but scrolls. A similar practice, which apparently continues to this day, is the Chinese method of indicating the size of a library's collection in *chüan*, or in other words in the fascicles of which each book is made up.

 14

Conflagrations

IN a letter to the emperor Manuel I (1143–1180), the learned John Tzetzes tells of a dream, or nightmare, which lasted all through a long night of disturbed sleep. To begin with, he was besieged and attacked (in his dream) by an army of fleas 'more numerous than the host which Xerxes led into Europe'. Then, towards dawn, he seemed to catch sight of a book in the hands of an artisan. The artisan was sitting outside a perfumer's shop, and the book, the *Scythian History* of Dexippus of Athens, was one which John particularly wanted and had never been able to obtain. (Dexippus, an aristocrat of ancient lineage, had gone out to confront the marauding Heruli beneath the city walls during the tempestuous third century.) But to the eye of the nightmare-ridden librarian, the precious book appeared to have been licked by flames: its parchment leaves were curled by the heat, the binding which should have held together the five-leaved gatherings dangled in wretched disarray. Nonetheless, the 'divine writing' had survived and was clearly visible (*Epistula* 58). The longed-for book, by now impossible to find and very probably destroyed forever, thus appeared in a dream to the scholar who coveted it, as if emerging once more from the flames that had engulfed it.

The history of the libraries of antiquity often ends in flames. Fire, along with earthquakes, is said by Galen to be one of the commonest causes of the destruction of books (XV: Kühn's ed. p. 24). Fires do not spring up without cause. It is as if a greater force were intervening to destroy an organism that could no longer be controlled or checked: impossible to check the infinite capacity for growth that libraries displayed, impossible to control their contents given the equivocal (often forged) nature of the material that poured into them.

It is hard to trace the genesis of this idea that libraries ended up in flames. Its distant origins may lie in a more or less clear perception of the fate suffered by the libraries of the great eastern kingdoms, where the inevitable fire which at length engulfed the 'palace' generally destroyed the adjoining library too. This library was remote, the exclusive property of the king, set apart and impenetrable to most people – as in the Ramesseum, where it lurked in the recesses of the monumental tomb, or the Museum, where it was placed within the Ptolemies' well fortified palace. Eventually, and anachronistically, an image of this kind was projected back onto a community like Athens, where for a long time no library in fact existed: Zosimus, we have seen, actually claimed to know that the supposed 'library of Athens' had gone up in flames at some unspecified point in Demosthenes' life.

Unverified assertions that this or that library was consumed by fire often refer to successive conflagrations at a single site. This is true of both Alexandria and Antioch – where the Museum, we are told, went up in flames under Tiberius and again under Jovian.

Traditions of this kind were confirmed by the melancholy experiences of the war waged by Christianity against the old culture and its sanctuaries: which meant, against the libraries. Here was a third destructive factor. Gibbon draws a picture of the archbishop Theophilus attacking the Serapeum, and this one scene can stand for many others. Theophilus, Gibbon relates with gentlemanly disgust,

> proceeded to demolish the temple of Serapis, without any other difficulties than those which he found in the weight and solidity of the materials; but these obstacles proved so insuperable, that he was obliged to leave the foundations; and to content himself with reducing the edifice itself to a heap of rubbish, a part of which was soon afterwards cleared away, to make room for a church, erected in honour of the Christian martyrs. The valuable library of Alexandria was pillaged or destroyed; and near twenty years afterwards, the appearance of the empty shelves excited the regret and indignation of every spectator, whose mind was not wholly darkened by religious prejudice [the reference is to Orosius] .... While the images and vases of gold and silver were carefully melted, and those of a less valuable metal were contemptuously broken, and cast into the streets, Theophilus laboured to expose the frauds and the vices of the ministers of the idols ... (Gibbon, 1838 ed., Vol. III, pp. 520–521).

The burning of books was part of the advent and imposition of Christianity. Malalas, the Antiochene chronicler,

describes another scene, under Justinian and in the capital of the Empire, which had numerous parallels: 'in the month of June of the same indiction, several Greeks [that is, pagans] were arrested and taken forcibly from place to place, and their books were burned in the *Kynegion* and so were the images and statues of their miserable gods' (Bonn ed., p. 491). The *Kynegion* was the place where the corpses of those condemned to death were flung.

15

Epilogue

IN 357 AD, the rhetorician Themistius expressed his
fears for the future of the classical texts. Themistius,
a sedulous Aristotelian commentator and a senator in the
new capital, was praising Constantius' initiative in founding
an imperial library at Byzantium; and he took the opportunity of underlining how necessary such an undertaking was.
Without it, he urged, the great classics would be in serious
peril (*Panegyric of Constantius*, pp. 59^d – 60^c). This was not
the first time the guardians of imperial power had mounted
an emergency programme to prevent the disappearance of
books. Domitian (81–96 AD) had decided at the start of
his reign to 'rebuild the libraries that had been burned',
and had accordingly 'had the whole empire searched for
copies of works that had disappeared' and 'sent emissaries
to Alexandria charged with copying and correcting the
texts' (Suetonius, *Life of Domitian*, 20). By the time of
Themistius, however, in the middle of the 4th century,
Constantius' initiative seemed a desperate last resort. The
cycle inaugurated seven centuries ago by the first Ptolemy
seemed to be drawing to a close.

In the Hellenistic-Roman world, there had been many

libraries, but they had been ephemeral. The small city and regional libraries, as well as the great centres, had been emblems – like the hot baths and the gymnasia – of a proud *civilitas* now engulfed in the anarchy of war.

Hadrian's library at Athens was among the first of the major libraries to come under attack. It was laid waste by the Heruli, who encountered relatively little resistance as they struck at the heart of the empire (267 AD). Alexandria's turn came a few years later. Indeed, it was now, in the course of the struggle between Zenobia and Aurelian, that the great library really met its end: Alexandria, wrote Ammianus, 'now lost the quarter called Bruchion which had long been the dwelling of the foremost men' (*amisit regionem quae Bruchion appellabatur, diuturnum praestantium hominum domicilium:* XXII, 16, 15). In this same quarter, wrote Epiphanius a few years later, where the library had once been, 'there is now a desert' (*Patrologia Graeca,* 43, 252). In a world afflicted by the frailty of the books which it produced, Alexandria had enjoyed a rare continuity. Traces of its activity are found almost up to the last moment. Some twenty years after Caesar's Alexandrian war, Strabo visited the Museum and described it. Half a century later, the emperor Claudius (41–54 AD), an antiquarian of great erudition, had a new Museum built alongside the old one in Alexandria (Suetonius, *Life of Claudius,* 42). Forty years after this, Domitian (81–96 AD) one of the worst of his successors, sent emissaries to Alexandria to make copies of the city's priceless books.

There is direct documentary evidence, too. For example,

we possess a private written agreement connected with the sale of a vessel on 31 March of the year 173 AD, signed by a certain Valerius Diodorus who describes himself as 'ex-vice librarian and member of the Museum' (Papyrus Merton, 19). Finally, early in the third century, we have the scholarly compilation of Athenaeus of Naucratis (in the Egyptian Delta): the learned conversations which convey the author's erudition may be imagined as taking place in Rome, but they leave no doubt that his native land was well supplied with books.

By the middle of the fourth century, even Rome was virtually devoid of books. Not long before Themistius's speech in praise of Constantius, the former capital's libraries had been closed – 'closed forever, like tombs' was the horrified comment of Ammianus (XIV, 6, 18). The newly reopened library at Antioch seems to have perished in a fire soon after this.

Surveying this series of foundations, refoundations and disasters, we follow a thread that links together the various, and mostly vain, efforts of the Hellenistic-Roman world to preserve its books. Alexandria is the starting point and the prototype; its fate marks the advent of catastrophe, and is echoed in Pergamum, Antioch, Rome, Athens. At Byzantium there was to be one last reincarnation – a palace library, once again, in the palaces of the emperor (Zosimus, III, 11, 3) and the patriarch (George of Pisis, carmen 46).

The great concentrations of books, usually found in the

centres of power, were the main victims of these destructive outbreaks, ruinous attacks, sackings and fires. The libraries of Byzantium proved no exception to the rule. In consequence, what has come down to us is derived not from the great centres but from 'marginal' locations, such as convents, and from scattered private copies.

Index